Mark...
I think you'll get a
kick out of this one.
(you're in it!) 🖂:

Eugene Saint

The Eggless Club

By Eugene Saint

The Eggless Club

February 2009
All rights reserved.
Copyright © 2009 by Eugene Saint

ISBN 9781441446251

Cover Design by J. L. Saint

To Dad
(Who plays the character of "My Old Man")
and...

To Mom
(Who plays the character of "My Old Lady")

And, of course, this book was written
For my wonderful wife...

Jennifer

Only the little kid in us survives each stage of life...that's only if you're lucky. I'm lucky.

Saint

TABLE OF CONTENTS

1

A Word About My Old Man

My old man is a funny guy. Great sense of humor. The funniest guy I've ever known. Except for some things. For one: we call him Dad, other folks call him Bob. If he ever heard me refer to him as "my old man" he'd, well — just don't do it.

His life is worse than mine. Not in a *grew up working in a sweatshop* sorta way or anything like that, but in a *if you think a lot of stuff is funny then it's occasionally gonna bite you* sorta way — thus saddling you with great one-liners that you'd damn well better keep to yourself else you're going to regret it — big time. Such was my old man's curse and he passed it on to me. It's a living hell.

Take for instance the winter we spent in Sault Saint Marie. Sault Saint Marie (pronounced *Soo* Saint Marie — strike one) is situated on the Upper Peninsula of Michigan. There, straddling the U.S./Canadian border, you'll find the Sault Locks (pronounced *Soo* Locks) — a set of locks designed and constructed to allow shipping traffic to pass between Lake Superior and Lake Huron. The entire winter we lived there the locks remained frozen solid. Few things in this world are more boring to a kid than frozen locks (strike two). Plus, it seemed like everybody spoke French (strike three) so this place wasn't even *trying* to get along with me.

One cold winter morning not long after we arrived in town Dad took my older brother Ronald and me to register at the local elementary school. In those days it was common practice upon arriving at a new school to just wander the halls until you found what you were looking for. It turns out, the registration office was on the second floor (that's kinda weird already, right?) so up the stairs we went. Sort of.

A few steps up, it struck all three of us at about the same time that each step, though of normal width and depth, was barely two inches high. It must have taken a hundred steps to get to the second floor. I looked at my brother. He looked at me — jaw dropping in an exaggerated expression of amazement. My brother is the Debil. Dad looked at both of us. He *knew*. He just *knew*. Like swinging on a rope you know is too rotted and frayed to hold you and sure enough, it doesn't. Things started to get funny.

Ronny and I (and no doubt Dad) were on our best behavior and did make it to the top of the stairway without incident although I do recall beginning to feel a little shocky. Here we faced a long long totally empty hallway (all the other kids were in class) covered with the kind of old battleship linoleum one sees in long long totally empty hallways of that era — waxed and polished over the years to a glass-hard reflection. Naturally the registration office was at the far end so that's where we headed — my brother and I side-by-side, the old man taking point.

Of course, the clack and clatter of our hard-soled shoes echoed and resonated throughout the building (not unlike banging garbage can lids in a cave) announcing our presence well in advance such that, as we passed each classroom, rows and columns of indigenous kids stared out at us like zombies (strike four).

One teacher, being somewhat more aware than the others, dragged her lecture to her door, closing it just in time before we passed — all without missing a beat. Other teachers (probably rookies) didn't and it was these *others* who compelled my brother to break into his sure-fire Hunchback Of Notre Dame routine just as we transited each doorway. Oh, he's good alright. Still, I managed to maintain my composure. It wasn't over yet.

Having successfully negotiated the gauntlet of classrooms, Dad shot us a *look* that sat my brother Ronny and me on a long ice-cold bench across the hall from the registration office. There we would wait while he went in. What a relief. We'd made it — so it would seem.

You have to understand, my old man has been a professional jazz drummer his entire life — that's how we ended up spending the winter in Sault Saint Marie (pronounced "Soo" Saint Marie) to begin with. The significance of this is that he had always been in pretty good physical shape and could outrun kids much faster than my brother or me. That meant if you screwed up bad and needed to get away, your only hope would be to make your move *early*.

But speed wasn't the only weapon in my old man's arsenal. In addition to possessing general overall speed he was lightning quick (there's a big difference) and deadly accurate with either hand. Once he got his hand on you, either one, it was too late. If you've ever been in the grasp of a six-foot lobster then you know what I'm talking about — escape is impossible short of gnawing off a body part.

Still...so far so good.

Dad seemed to take forever in the registration office and that was a good thing. The long ice-cold bench was working its magic — dragging my brother and me ever back from that hard edge of comic hysteria seldom more than a misstep away back in those days.

Eventually Dad came back out and sat next to us on the ice-cold bench — he no doubt needed it too. Seemed we had to wait for a "Mrs. Lafleur" (strike five) who would "be with us shortly".

Usually when someone "will be with you shortly" it means they won't — but this time proved the exception so let's take a moment to differentiate *real* time from *apparent* time.

The gist of it is this: Real time is measured with a clock. Apparent time is measured in events. Now, that might sound simple enough on paper but allow me to share with you the real-life in-your-face example as it was presented to me on that cold winter day in Sault Saint Marie (pronounced "Soo" Saint Marie), Michigan.

Click. Click. Click.

Somebody's coming up the steps at the far end of the hall.

Click. Click. Click.

High heels. Probably green. Probably Mrs. Lafleur.

Click. Click. Click. Click. Click.

Those ridiculous two-inch steps. Way too many.

Click. Click. Click. Click. Click.

Like remembering the punch line of a good joke. Those ridiculous steps. No problem. I can handle it. Must handle it...

The top of her head rises above the top of the stairway. It is Mrs. Lafleur.

Click. Click. Click. Click. Click.

It's not working. Too many steps. Not enough incremental rise per step. Apply deviation for goofy steps. Factor in parallax. Still not working.

Click click. Click click. Click click.

Now she has crested the stairway and is heading our way. Dad rises, trying to look responsible. The scene is *way* too serious. Sporting a rainbow of troweled-on makeup, Mrs. LaFleur is about four feet wide but stands only about three feet tall. She's getting closer but it doesn't seem to make any difference. What's up with that? She's the object that "appears farther away in this mirror". Things are serious. Too serious. Funny serious and my reality has become a centrifuge...

5 G's, 6 G's...

Space-time is beginning to warp...

Click click. Click click. Click click.

Must maintain. My older brother looking at me — jaw dropped in exaggerated amazement. Must maintain, Debil or no...

7 G's...

Click click. Click click. Click click.

Closer. Closer — but no bigger. Green high heels (strike whatever)...

Click click. Click click. Click click.

10...11 G's...I'm leaving my body...

12 ...13...14 G's...

Hovering near the ceiling — a father below. Clenched teeth. Barely audible. Lips not moving. Poking two kids (one regular and one Debil) in the chest with only one finger on one lobster claw and saying, "Not. One. Word! Do you understand me?! Not. One. Word!" Eyes saying, "Dammit, this is not going to work. Dammit."

Click click.   Click click.   Click click.

15...16 G's!

Time approaching zero — mass approaching infinity...

Click click.   Click click.   Click click.

Blackout.

I awoke hundreds of years later in the back seat of a Desoto — registered in an elementary school in a town that can't spell its own name. A town where, that very winter, eight people died — their bodies crushed and horribly mangled by massive icicles falling from tall office buildings.

Yeah, my old man's a funny guy...and now I've got it.

2

The Eggless Club and Munk's Corner

Columbus, Ohio. My hometown. Actually, I grew up outside of Columbus in what was — back then anyway — way out in the country. There they had put in a few streets and a handful of houses in what would probably be called a sub-division nowadays. From my neighborhood we could practically watch the big city heading our way.

This particular place was known, at least in those days, as Munk's Corner because first and foremost it was a corner — in fact it was the intersection of Refugee Road and Old Route 33 — and secondly, because Old Man Munk owned it. He'd built a truck stop there about a thousand years ago and settled in for the long haul. I don't recall ever seeing more than a couple trucks there at any one time but, then again, I don't recall ever seeing less than a couple trucks there either.

Naturally, we weren't allowed to hang out at Munk's Corner but we'd find different reasons to go there anyway. I remember cigarettes were only twenty-three cents a pack and my old man would give me a quarter to run and get him a pack of Camel non-filters — Luckys if they're out of Camels — and I'd get to keep the change. At the time it was, financially speaking, a worthwhile venture. On a good day you could find three or four pop bottles along the mile or so stretch of country road between our house and Munk's Corner. More if you went the long way. Old Man Munk took pop bottles. Two cents each — cash.

We'd always enter through the screen door in the back. Old Man Munk didn't want us using the regular front entrance because he sold beer (and kids couldn't be in a place where they sold beer) so I'm guessing it was kind of a secret and Old Man Munk didn't want to press his luck.

Munk's Corner had a pinball machine. I remember it had pictures of pretty girls wearing hardly anything at all and they would light up from time to time depending upon some conditional logic I was never quite able to grasp. I know it had something to do with the total score but sometimes when I thought they should light up — they didn't. That was a shame too because when they did light up, the girls magically lost what little clothing they had. Worth waiting for.

I never knew exactly how all of that worked, just that every once in a while some trucker on the machine would whoop, "Hot damn!" the pretty girls would lose their garb and some money would change hands between Old Man Munk and the lucky winner. Apparently all of that stuff was illegal too — depending mostly on the current county sheriff and who Old Man Munk had supported in the most recent election.

Old Man Munk never minded us boys hanging around — within reason of course — except sometimes when certain folks would pull into the truck stop. Then he'd turn to us and say, "You boys git," and we'd git.

In the meantime, the six or eight cents worth of pop bottle deposit money coupled with the two cent cigarette delivery fee amounted to a pretty hefty chunk of change when it came to four-for-a-penny candy. We'd usually hang around until it was all spent then we'd take my old man his smokes and head up to our clubhouse in anticipation of the impending sugar high.

We had probably the world's best clubhouse. It was originally built as a chicken coop and was the last remnant of a long gone farm. The rest of the farm had burned down years before anybody we knew moved to the area and now the entire forty or fifty acres were covered with tall weeds. Great weeds. The kind of weeds you could stomp a network of paths through then by following the paths you could get *from* anywhere *to* anywhere without being seen. That's a big deal to kids. Not only that, these were the kind of weeds that would turn white and stiff in the fall — perfect for building forts.

For many many years the old chicken coop had been a clubhouse — handed down from one generation of kids to the next. Kids known now only by their initials carved randomly throughout the structure. Kids who probably grew up, left, and died in wars and stuff. Even the original coop had been constructed from old wood that had previously been part of something else — you could tell by the rust-fringed nail holes and peeling paint in places that otherwise didn't make sense.

It had, over the years, undergone sufficient repairs and minor upgrades to remain fairly dry except for the far back corner. That was home to too many spiders to really mess with. All in all, a great clubhouse.

If you want to get technical, it began — as was clearly painted on the door — as the "Eagles Club" but here's what I think happened: Whoever painted that name didn't realize that the word "Eagles" contains an "a". Someone must have pointed that out right off the bat because an obvious attempt at correcting the first "g" to make it into an "a" resulted in a lower case "a" with kind of a tail. Black oil-base paint is not very forgiving.

To make matters worse, in order to make the word possessive plural an extra "s" had been added. The final product looked more like "Eggless" than anything else. Whoever it was (remember I'm just guessing here) must have been a big kid and after a couple "I meant that, I meant that"s and possibly a punch or two, the spelling was allowed to stand. That's *my* take on it anyway. As good a way as any for a legend to begin I suppose.

So, "Eggless" Club it was — and the name stuck. Thus, we were stuck with it and naturally felt obliged to defend our club's name as though it was a cool one.

The big city has long since expanded well beyond my old stomping grounds but, at least the last time I drove by, the Eggless clubhouse remains standing, surrounded by a field of great weeds. A lost world, having long fallen off the county land assessor's books. Like one of those skinny triangles of land left over at the edge of a township when they try to reconcile physical acreage with straight longitudinal lines juxtaposed on a round planet. A no less historical site than Jamestown or Antietam or any other place as far as I'm concerned.

3

Storm Drains

We didn't care much for the Catholics — at least at first. It wasn't really their fault. In fact, their problems began long before they even moved into the neighborhood. So, "How is that possible?" you might ask.

The truth is, we didn't know the first thing about Catholics. I suppose we knew they actually existed but I wouldn't even swear to that. Not unlike other peoples I know nothing about, I can't honestly say I had an opinion one way or the other — pro or con.

The Catholics' problem began when somebody sold (and somebody bought) the tract of land between Bobby Stafford's backyard and the Bolls farm.

We were sure it hadn't belonged to Old Man Bolls because he'd always plowed and planted every square foot of his acreage — every year — and this particular parcel of land was, and had been, completely overgrown with tall weeds for as far back as we could remember. The soil consisted of a light brown loam with high clay content. If, as most farmers agree, the best soil is the dark fertile stuff then this dirt was totally worthless — unless, of course, your intention was to grow really great weeds. For that, it proved superb.

Unlike grass or wheat or just about anything else, really great weeds don't provide much defense against soil erosion. Situated on a reasonably steep grade, the hydraulic action of many rainy seasons had streaked the slope from top to bottom with deep gullies. Gullies culminating in a drainage ditch running from the edge of Old Man Bolls' farm all the way to Alum Creek. Following this ditch was how we ultimately discovered Alum Creek to begin with — but that's another story.

Several of the steep-sided trenches were deep enough to stand up in without being seen — rivaling even some of the arroyos found in the Great Southwest. During any rainstorm, big chunks of the rain-saturated walls would collapse into the gullies. Subsequent torrents of water would, like a mining sluice, wash away the dirt, silt and particulate matter, leaving in their wake a fresh batch of newly revealed stuff — rocks and minerals along with an occasional arrowhead and possibly even (what we figured could only be) Indian teeth.

The morning after any good storm (storms always happen at night you know) you would find us kids scouring the gullies for new — and conceivably really cool — collectibles. Then one day all of that changed.

Early one morning my mother woke me up. "Bobby's here," she said. Her concern was obvious. "I think there's something wrong."

Hopping up, I ran to the living room to find Bobby Stafford, nearly in tears.

"What's up, man?"

"They're killing our field!"

Barefoot, standing there in my pajamas, I wasn't quite sure what he had said but Bobby was already out the door and running toward his house. The next thing I knew, Mom was straightening my hair with one hand and giving me the bum's rush toward the door with the other, yelling, "Go! Just go!" (I've always thought that was pretty cool — for a girl) and I took off up the hill after Bobby. Cutting through backyards and hopping fences, I caught up with him standing in his own backyard, staring out into the field — or rather, what had *been* the field.

The place was lousy with bulldozers, earthmovers and all sorts of heavy construction equipment — digging and scraping and pushing more dirt around in a single pass than the lot of us kids could have in a whole year. Guys in hardhats were everywhere — yelling back and forth to each other just to be heard over the cacophony of huge machine beasts. Some of them were walking around pointing to different spots along the ground and every so often planting long triangular wooden stakes. It was horrible, like bearing witness to the massacre at Wounded Knee. We were devastated.

At one point a worker came to within twenty feet of us and erected a tripod to hold the tiniest telescope I'd ever seen. He was trying to get a good look at some other guy standing on the opposite side of the field holding a long white ruler.

"Hey mister, whatcha doin'?"

The man looked up, all smiles, "We're gonna build a road."

"What for?"

"They're gonna put in some new houses. You're gonna have some new neighbors." Still all smiles.

Off course our knee-jerk reaction begged we defend our turf. Bobby and I looked around our immediate vicinity but his back yard was devoid of any good throwing-rocks. We mentally estimated the distance from us to our field — now laden with freshly made dirt clods — and back to Bobby's house. The odds were against us — way against us. All the other workers, besides this idiot with the tripod, looked huge and we instinctively knew if we allowed ourselves to become encircled, we'd be dead meat.

I guess that's a good thing. Bobby and I would probably still be sharing a prison cell. Besides, the damage was already done. It's times like these when you realize you're only on this planet for a short while. There's no time to wallow in self-pity.

Sitting in his backyard swilling Kool-Aid, Bobby and I and reminisced about the good times and the many, many hours we'd spent extracting the treasures from those wonderful ditches. Those geological marvels.

One by one our remaining club members arrived. It was the same thing each time. First disbelief and denial. Then anger followed by grief and eventually acceptance — in that order.

So no, it wasn't exactly the Catholics' fault but it is they who would get the blame. Yeah, life ain't fair...tell me about it.

Unfair as it is, somehow life went on — with each passing day the field looking less and less like it had and more and more like it does now. Before long it was hard to even remember what it used to look like at all. You can never go home.

I have to admit, watching the big machines toil had its merit. All day long the earthmovers, looking like huge yellow dinosaurs, would lumber along scraping up great mounds of earth with their bellies. Then they'd go to the other end of the tract and, with the pull of a lever, the belly would open up — releasing the dirt in a long even layer as the machine headed back for another gulp. One of the drivers even let me climb up and drive his earthmover one day. Sitting on the seat, I got to steer while he controlled all the other stuff. Did you know those things don't even have steering wheels? They just have a metal bar with a big button at each end. If you push one — it turns right. If you push the other one — it turns left. Outrageously cool. I still want one.

After the earthmovers had made a few passes, other guys would come along behind, compacting the dirt with steamrollers. That part would ultimately be the new road. Actually, they were making two roads: one parallel with our street, extending an older neighborhood from the top of the hill to the bottom of the hill — and a second new road that would "T" off the first one — one end connecting to our street, the other dead-ending at the Bolls farm.

A few weeks into the project the earthmovers were replaced by steam shovels. Brontosaurs swapped out for T-Rex's, whole different animals altogether. These creatures came to cut notches in the ground along either side of the new roads — the houses to be built on these lots being of the split-level type.

After notching the half-basements identified with split-level construction they (this is important) cut deep trenches alongside the two new streets. The trench that connected to the "T" at the bottom of the hill was extended all the way past the new houses-to-be — to the field beyond. Concrete boxes were then planted at various points along the trenches.

What makes this important is: the boxes were then plumbed together with 2-foot diameter concrete pipes, thus creating a network of storm runoff drains. Networks of 2-foot diameter concrete pipes are great when you're a kid because you fit inside them. We just called them the tunnels.

The arrangement was such that a kid entering the drainage system from the field could crawl to just about anywhere in the new housing complex — popping up at any of five different egress points: One at the T. One at each end of that street. One in the middle of the hill and one at the top.

No matter how hot it got outside, the tunnels remained nice and cool all summer. While the openings provided pretty good light at the ends, stuff doesn't get much darker than it does in the middle of those things. Still, it's not like you could get lost or anything and it's amazing how little light is required to illuminate such a dark place.

Being new and all, the pipes were devoid of spiders and creepy stuff so that was good. Don't get me wrong, spiders are alright — granted, little ones are better than the big fuzzy ones — but they're a lot easier to cope with in some place other than dark, limited access, buried concrete tubes.

Of course, like any really cool place, the tunnels were not without inherent drawbacks. Obviously, it was cramped. Some kids, like Eddie, could only go a little ways into the tunnels before having to get out immediately. He said he was claustrophobic — which I believe is Latin for *chicken*.

Another problem with the concrete tubes was — you couldn't turn around. In order to go back the way you came in, you had to either back up all the way or go to one of the access points, turn around and crawl back.

The same thing applied when another kid was between you and where you wanted to be. To be honest, it is technically possible to pass by another kid in the middle of the tunnel but that involves one kid lying extremely flat while the other kid squeezes by. Bobby and I nearly got stuck doing that one time. It even made me feel claustrophobic. In fact, it can be downright freaky. I can tell you one thing: no matter how hard you push, concrete pipe buried five feet underground won't budge. You don't want to think about that part too much. That was the last time we ever attempted that maneuver.

In many ways, the network of drainage pipes that came with the new housing development made up for the loss of one field — even a good field. We still had plenty of other fields but how many kids do you know with their own subterranean passageway to anywhere?

Of course, knowing our parents' immediate reaction would be "stay out of the pipes" we didn't tell them about the tunnels right away. It didn't take long though for Moms to take notice of our jeans. In addition to being extremely hard on the kneecaps, crawling around inside concrete tubes will wear a hole through your pants quicker than that lady from the Coney Island Washboard Roundelay. It seemed our Moms were forever ironing on new patches.

Eventually one Mom got to talking with another Mom and...you can probably guess the rest. The word was out — it was dangerous. The network of tunnels was added to our growing list of off-limits stuff. We even tried to talk Bill's Mom into crawling up into the pipes just to see first-hand how safe they really were but she wouldn't. She claimed she wouldn't fit but she didn't fool us for one minute with that lame excuse. She was plum chicken. She was a girl and she was plum chicken — end of story.

After that, we just had to be careful not to be seen entering or leaving the pipes — no big deal. Once out of the tunnel it would be hard to prove we'd been in there. Once inside the tunnel, we could be reasonably certain no one was going to come crawling in looking for us. The last few feet of pipe dropped off rather sharply where it emptied into the drainage ditch and once you were in past the bend it was impossible to be seen by someone looking in from outside.

In fact, one day my mother sent my old man to see if we were in there. He came to the end of the pipes and yelled, "You boys in there?"

We didn't make a sound — didn't breathe — but he didn't wait long before we could hear him turn and walk away, calling back to Mom, "No, Honey. They're not down here."

I think he knew we were there. Knew, but didn't care. None of the men cared. I think they would have crawled up in there with us but they truly didn't fit. Dads are cool like that.

One Sunday about a month after school was back in session I'd backed in and crawled backwards all the way to the middle. Bobby followed me in, head first, scooting a little piece of plywood nearly as wide as the pipe, in front of him as he went. Once in the middle, the plywood served as an excellent table — spanning the lower part of the pipe. There we lit a candle, pulled out a deck of cards and played "Go Fish".

It had been sprinkling when we entered the tunnel but no matter. The water simply ran in a small stream along the bottom of the pipes. It was cool really. On our hands and knees straddling the middle of the pipe is how we normally were anyway. The only other legitimate positions were either layng on your belly (propped up on your elbows) or on your back staring at the ceiling.

Bobby, after a couple of hours of complaining about his knees being sore, decided to call it a day. I on the other hand, had about six layers of knee patches and was perfectly comfortable. Bobby backed away and out of sight. When he got to the end of the pipe, he yelled back that it was starting to rain pretty hard. Then he left. Dealing the cards, I thought, "Cool...all the more reason to stick around."

The rest of the afternoon I sat, or rather knelt, playing War to see who would win (me or me), thinking if I waited awhile the rain might subside. After a couple hours or so I could tell by the water passing by that it hadn't. No big deal. After all, we had spent many a rainy day goofing around up in the pipes, dry as bones.

Eventually I got bored with beating myself at War and decided the day was just about over. The last thing I wanted was to climb out of the tunnel only to find it completely black outside. Think about it, exactly how do you explain away that you were out past dark because *you didn't know it was dark?* Exactly. Packing up my cards and putting them, along with the candle, back into my pockets — I crawled toward the exit.

Nearing what should have been the exit, I realized something wasn't right. Having crawled that length of tunnel many times, I had a good sense of where in the tunnel *I ought to be by now* but something was wrong. It should have been getting lighter but it wasn't.

I continued forward in the dark — my mind busy trying to come up with some believable excuse for having misread the whole planet turning dark — when SPLAT! I hit water.

Backing up, I pulled out the candle and lit it. Bobby was right. It had been raining harder. A lot harder. The swollen drainage ditch had crested its banks and the storm drain had filled up past the bend. I could see the pipe ahead of me curve downward then plunge beneath the waterline. Not good.

So, exactly how far was it to the opening? Ten feet? Fifteen feet? I knew how far it was, right? I was sure how far it was, right? But how sure? *That's where they'll find the body* sure? What if something's blocking the end of the pipe? Could I make it back? How much of a good swimming stroke can you get trying to swim backward inside a two-foot diameter concrete pipe that won't budge no matter how hard you push?

Even in the short while I'd spent contemplating those questions and more, the water had risen visibly. I decided my best bet would be to back up all the way to the T and climb out there.

It was a long way and seemed to take forever. I could feel the new patches on my knees beginning to wear thin. Eventually, I looked back over my shoulder and saw the tunnel begin to lighten from what little sunshine was provided by the rainy overcast sky. Great. My world was literally brighter. My relief was short-lived.

As I backed out into the open space of the concrete box denoting the T, ice-cold water was washing in from the other pipes intersecting the node. I expected that. More ice-cold water poured in from the swales above. I expected that too. What I hadn't expected was what I saw when I looked up.

Since the last time I (or any of us kids) had been there, someone had come along and installed a heavy metal grate over the egress. Not just put it there, mind you, but put it there *and* cemented it into place!

Hard as I tried, I couldn't budge it any more than I could budge the concrete pipes.

I needed a plan C. While the water pouring in from the pipes to my left and right was slow moving, it was also deep. Too deep. So, I could either stand there and call for help in the middle of a rainstorm at the intersecting T of two streets lined with empty houses or; I could continue up the hill. There were two more possible exits — one halfway up the hill, the other at the top — so continue up the hill I did.

My knees were killing me by the time I reached what turned out to be another grate cemented into place. This exit point was made up of a concrete box set into the ground with one pipe leading into it and one pipe leading out. The box was shallower than back at the "T" but — even laying on my back in the ice-cold water and pushing with my legs — I couldn't budge the metal grate. My only hope was to continue moving up the hill.

By now my knees were beginning to shred. Even the tiniest imperfection in the concrete pipe would send jolts of pain through my whole leg. My matches were soaked. My candle — mere dead weight. I kept going.

Crawling as much on my hands as on my knees I got to the top of the hill where the pipe leveled off again. That helped. I was freezing, tired, my knees were bloody, and I was on the verge of giving up as I dragged myself into the concrete box at the end of the pipeline — the end of the road.

It was the end of the road, alright. Literally. It was, in fact, the end of the new road and the beginning of the old road. That meant the only pipe coming or going was the one I had just come through and this exit too had been grated over.

The concrete box here was different than the others, though. For one thing, it was shallow. More importantly, the metal grate was also of a different type. It not only had the prison-looking bars of the other ones on top but also had a rectangular slot along the side facing the old neighborhood — like the kind they use for curbs. The opening was probably three feet wide but only about eight inches high.

It took a lot of effort but I was able to push with my legs off the opposite wall and force my head through the opening. Now, not only were my ears killing me but at one point I could no longer reach the back wall with my feet. With water damming up all around my face, for one horrific moment I thought, "Oh great, so *this* is how they're going to find me." That's when I managed to get one last good grip on the metal frame and pull myself half way through.

Pam and Beverly Carter lived in the last house on the older section of street. I remember laying on my back in the ice-cold rainwater, propped on my elbows, and seeing Pam and Beverly standing in the bay window of their living room watching me struggling to climb out of the storm drain. Obviously excited about the whole thing, they ran off — no doubt to get somebody.

By the time Old Man Carter opened his front door I had wriggled free of the grate and was running down the street. I'm sure he thought, "Hmmph, just boys goofing around," and went back inside.

When I got home, Mom freaked out. I told her the whole story. Well, most of it anyway. The only thing I changed was, I told her I'd suddenly remembered leaving my beloved deck of playing cards in the storm drain long before it was verboten to go in there and was just going to retrieve them when it started raining.

She bought it and, after a couple "I told you so"s, insisted I eat some hot soup.

My old man was asleep on the couch throughout the recounting of my tale of near tragedy. The Browns had lost to the Steelers. Sleeping on the couch was his way of coping with a Cleveland loss.

The tunnels weren't much fun in the winter. Not only did the cold wind funnel through the tubes and the concrete literally suck the heat from your body but the daily freeze/thaw weather conditions common to Ohio guaranteed a constant trickle of ice water. We didn't go into the drainage pipes much that winter and come spring they were lined with six inches of mud. By then creepy critters much worse than spiders had aced us out of our digs.

We had traded a great field of weeds and gullies for an outrageously cool subterranean network of passageways. It had been a great experience and fun — mostly. If you ever have the opportunity to crawl through a bunch of concrete tubes, don't pass it up.

By the time school let out for the summer the tunnels were defunct — at least as far as little kids were concerned — but we still had our fields.

4

Dirt Clod Fighting and Catholics

I grew up surrounded by fields. Cornfields, soybean fields, pumpkins, turnips, some just plain open fields. You never knew until late spring or so what kind of field you we're gonna get that year. That's important to a kid. I mean, one year you'd have corn — tall, good for hiding. You can run down a ways, cut over a few rows and you're gone. In a cornfield, little kids actually have the advantage over big kids — at least for the latter half of the summer until the harvest. By then the stalks are tall enough that a little kid can run underneath the leaves. If big kids tried that they'd get all cut up. Cornfields are great.

The next year that very same field might be turnips. Turnips are one of the worst. For the whole year that field would be considered "wide-open turf" and, as every kid knows, you never enter wide-open turf unless you are well out of dirt-clod range. Naturally there are exceptions, like intentionally drawing fire to reveal your opponents' position. Then there's the time Don low-crawled the length of Old Man Bolls' freshly plowed soybean field in a classic flanking maneuver — totally surprising the Catholics with a hail of dirt clods. Retreating in a full panic, the Catholics stampeded up through the old drainage ditch where, you guessed it, the rest of us kids were waiting. My God, it was a turkey shoot.

The Catholics were from another neighborhood. We, that is we in *our* neighborhood, were all pretty

24

much raised some kind of Protestant — Methodist? Presbyterian maybe? — so we didn't know a whole lot about the Catholics, just that they mostly lived a couple streets over and there were usually enough of them to get up a full team to play whatever it was we wanted to play, so it was cool. That they were stuck spending so much time in church and studying the Bible and so forth was just their tough luck. The general consensus amongst us non-Catholics was that all that Bible studying really limited the Catholics' ability to plan and execute the more elaborate tactical strikes necessary for modern dirt clod warfare — the kind of hard hitting, well organized, lightning fast guerilla strikes for which we in our neighborhood were well known and in which we took great pride.

Dirt clod fighting and just about everything else we played (other than your typical football, baseball and basketball — in that order) generally came under the heading of *playing army*. That way, whenever we found ourselves explaining to our parents how one of us got hurt it always seemed to go a little smoother if the explanation started with, "We were playing army and...." Seems folks are just naturally more sympathetic to a kid who gets hurt playing army than they are to a kid who gets hurt playing, say, full contact football with no helmet or pads. Oh, no. You get hurt playing football and it's, "Well, what did you expect?" and, "You'll live". Parents love it when you're standing there in pain and they can make you feel stupid too.

The whole idea of dirt clod fighting is to hit the other guy with dirt clods while not getting hit yourself. It sounds simple — and it fundamentally is simple — but there are rules — or rather some *unwritten* conventions that pretty much represent the whole of the law. The first rule is, "You don't intentionally try to hurt anyone." The object, of course, is to hit the other guy with dirt clods but ideally you want to hit him good enough to make him cuss but not bad enough to make him run home crying and subsequently rat you out. If they do squeal on you, you can squeal back on them for cussing. That probably won't help you much but at least they'll get a whipping too. *Yeah, well I'll tell your Mom you were cussin'* can be a robust deterrent to squealers, especially if you have a witness (whether your "witness" was actually there or not).

The second rule is, "You don't clobber a guy at point blank range." While on the surface this may seem a purely humanitarian caveat, it is in fact merely a reasonable construction based on the first rule. Again, you can't just stand there clobbering a guy or there's going to be trouble.

These two simple rules proved to be adequate, even through the *dark years*, and we never really lost anyone — though I would imagine to this day Dave still has problems seeing with that left eye of his.

These are the only agreed upon conventions of dirt clod fighting. How closely to which they are adhered (or how broadly they may be interpreted) is, more often than not, a question of good judgment. One must always factor in such specifics as "How big is the other kid?" "How fast is the other kid?" "How far away is the other kid?" and so on. These are zero tolerance, you'd better get it right the *first time*, lessons taught by dead kids.

On the other hand, one should not confuse such minimal bureaucracy with a lack of sophistication. Many a decision has been handed down vis-a-vis dirt clod tribunals wherein the outcomes of battles (and the territorial boundaries determined by those outcomes) have hinged entirely upon such details as weather conditions and dirt clod consistency at the time of the alleged incident.

For example, it had long been established fact that:

"...*freshly plowed* dirt clods yield a very dramatic explosion upon impact with the side of one's head — while a dirt clod *of equal size and weight* that had been *baking in the sun* all summer would *under the same circumstances* crush a guy's skull." [See: Bill v Dave ca. July 1957]

However, that decision would later be struck down and amended [See: Jimmy v Catholics ca. August 1957] wherein it was held that:

"...that same dirt clod *having been exposed to several days of rain — in August* is to be hereafter considered *exponentially less lethal* to the extent that the use of said dirt clod shall not be deemed a punishable offense beyond that of the *thrower* being considered a jerk."

Someone once defined diplomacy as: "The art of saying, 'nice doggie, nice doggie,' while you look for a big rock," and it was in the crucible of these dirt clod fights (and resultant tribunals) that I would not only develop but also hone to a razor's edge the diplomatic skill-set that would serve me so well in the waning days of that summer.

Dirt clod fighting lacks sophistication? I think not.

5

Big Kids

Here's the deal. There are *big* kids and *little* kids. Big kids are those kids who are two maybe even three grades ahead of little kids. It's a sliding window. No matter how old you get, you'll always be a little kid to them. Guys even bigger than that don't really matter too much as they are well outside a little kid's circle of influence — thus rendering them for the most part, moot beings. Regular *big* kids, on the other hand, are those kids who are bigger than you but who you do come into contact with on a semi-regular basis. *Big* kids.

When you're a little kid, that's mostly all you need to know about other kids. Are they big kids or little kids? You hear things like, "You know...what's-his-name, lives out on Watkins Road...big kid." *Big kid.* All you really need to know. Big kids can perform mathematical feats like adding and subtracting and knowing in advance how much change they're gonna get back. Little kids can't. Big kids know hemispheres and big words. Little kids don't. Two distinct camps.

There's no real transition period between being a little kid and being a big kid. Just one day you're standing there and a little kid asks you something that a little kid might ask a big kid and you're it. Suddenly you're a big kid and the weight of having to know all the stuff little kids know plus the big kid stuff too settles upon you like that dream where you're the only one who didn't know the test was today. A taste of real-world pressure. The kind of pressure that squeezes coal into diamonds. Now it's *you* who needs to know why eggs turn white when you cook them but don't turn clear again when they cool back down. It's *you* who needs to know, "If you're falling in an elevator and you jump up *just before it hits the ground*, will you make it?" Heady stuff. Don't let them see you sweat. Don't fold. Take the pain.

This is about the time you realize it's much better to be convincing than truthful and you say stuff like, "That's so you can tell if there's any eggshells in it," and, "Sure, my uncle knew a guy who did that and all he got was a broken leg. Everyone else got creamed."

If you're a little kid, you need to be constantly on your guard against sucker tricks by big kids, even those big kids you might consider friendlies. These tricks could range from the classic, "Go deep, go deep..." (then they turn around and walk off instead of throwing you the ball) to more elaborate, lesser known, second and third approximation tricks. One of the better ones — depending on one's point of view — was the time Bobby Stafford and I found a treasure map on the ground right next to our fort.

The fact that we hadn't noticed the map laying there when we built the fort earlier that morning never crossed our minds. The map sure looked genuine enough. It was labeled *"1851 — (before the Civil War)"* and everything. To top it off, one square drawn along the edge of the map was clearly marked *Start here at Bill's House*. Further instructions read:

Go straight across Bolls field to the mulberry tree. Go twenty paces up the ditch toward Casperson's. Dig.

I see now the three-hole spiral bound notebook paper should have alerted us to the map's fraudulent origin but it was too late. We were already drunk with the kind of greed and treasure-lust that accompanies the prospect of untold riches buried deep within Mother Earth — and it was just one field away from where we lived. Bobby and I set out to recon the situation.

Unfortunately, the patrol involved crossing the turnip field. Wide open turf. Not good. On the other hand, it had been the quietest week in recent memory along the battlefront. That's because some of the kids in my neighborhood were off visiting relatives. Bill was stuck at home with something that almost killed him — don't remember what. Something with a long name. He had been to the hospital but they'd sent him home. He wasn't allowed out and if he couldn't go out then his brothers couldn't either, at least that's what we gathered from it.

The Catholics had all gone to some kind of church camp including all but two of the Cassidi brothers. John (who they called Jack) and James (who they called Jim). There were a bunch of Cassidi brothers. Why these two hadn't gone with the others is a mystery but they were delighted to have stayed home.

As luck would have it, we knew *they* were all gone but they thought *we* were all there. Foreign intelligence is a wonderful thing. The fact is — the Catholic church-camp thing was a yearly event and we knew it. They knew we knew it and we knew they knew we knew it.

Jack and Jim Cassidi also knew the two of them alone could hardly withstand an all out assault not *if* but *when* it came. The pressure must have been tremendous. Bobby and I devised a plan. A plan so bold, so ingenious, so *in your face*, it is still (I'm told) talked about in some circles. In hallways and around campfires. Our finest hour.

Bobby and I stood up in plain sight and walked *casually* across the field! My heart was in my throat. I could hear my blood pumping. Be cool. Don't panic. Slow it down.

The Cassidis weren't falling for it. They refused to be baited. They *knew* it was just a trick and they weren't about to bite. We looked like we "looked like it wasn't a trick but really was". It worked. It actually worked. The real trick was — it wasn't a trick. The ultimate bluff.

Progressing across the wide open turnip field, our confidence growing with each step, I sensed a grin coming over my face and before long our gait had morphed into a full-blown strolling swagger. We even stopped at one point, kneeling to casually inspect a handful of the fertile loam — suggesting a keen understanding of that fine balance between soil nutrients and pH levels. Perhaps we would advise Old Man Bolls to adjust one or the other or both, with an eye toward maximizing crop yield on a per acre basis. Confident. Confidence that comes with knowing you're backed up by an army of kids (or a really big brother) hiding in wait — itching to pounce and destroy the instant a prearranged signal is given — the ensuing onslaught guaranteed to darken the sky with a rain of dirt clods on a scale dwarfing even that of the fabled "Turkey Shoot".

Thus, certain the gravity of their situation had been tamped home, we traversed the remainder of Old Man Bolls' turnip field — reaching the mulberry tree unchallenged.

By the way, mulberries technically grow on *bushes* not *trees*. At least this is the position vehemently defended by botanical professor types. Skewed opinions borne of academics laboring under the weight of decades of over-institutionalization.

Any kid worth his salt can tell you: Trees can be climbed — bushes can't. Simple as that. Had just *one* of the so-called experts ever pulled his egghead out of the books long enough to actually climb a tree then they'd know too. Hence the truism: those who can't, teach.

We picked and ate mulberries while analyzing the terrain. Then, after what seemed to be an adequate delay, we moseyed up the shallow drainage ditch in the direction of Casperson's market — maintaining a mental count of our steps. Thirty steps later (I was good at "tens") we stopped, studying the foliage lining the ditch for a couple minutes, before backtracking ten steps. To anyone struggling to grasp the reasoning behind this feint I won't bother to explain it because you're an idiot.

The spot depicted on the treasure map was, indeed, exactly where it should be. This was it! Directly below us lay the mother lode. Our luck didn't stop there. The ground beneath our feet was as hard as baked clay. Quite obviously this hiding place had remained unmolested since "before the Civil War".

The bad news was: it would be impossible to get to the treasure without proper earthmoving gear. This posed a very serious challenge. Bobby and I returned to the mulberry tree to pick more berries and contemplate our next move.

So far our strategy had worked even better than anticipated but Bobby and I both knew we didn't have a lot of time to play with. Catholics are, after all, notoriously unpredictable. We needed a shovel.

The good news was: we knew just where to procure one on short notice without arousing parental suspicion.

The bad news was: it was the Cassidis' old man's genuine U.S. Army entrenching tool. The Cassidis' old man had served in Korea and although he hadn't actually carried this particular genuine U.S. Army entrenching tool in the war — it was almost as good. The question was, "How to get it?"

The good news was: Jack and Jim were the youngest — and as such, the least valuable — of the Cassidi brothers when it came to things like choosing-up sides.

Throughout kiddom there are standard procedures employed to determine teams. These same procedures are typically used to decide such things as who will kick and who will receive. Who has "first bats". Who is "IT" first game, and so on. Well established time honored conventions that have evolved since the dawn of mankind. Since that time when it was first agreed upon that "first bounce" was as good as a "fly". When it was decided that along with "first picks" comes "last bats". Indelibly etched into our DNA. International in scope and applicability. "One potato, two potato..." translates seamlessly to "Uno papa, dos papa...". The single attribute shared by all of these conventions is their inherent fairness.

"Eenie meenie minie mo — you're out," means you're out. Done deal. Final and absolute. No appellate court in the world would ever so much as docket a challenge for consideration. It carries the full weight of history — trumping the Magna Carte and U.S. Constitution rolled into one. Beyond that lies anarchy. Why those methods of arbitration don't carry over into the *real world* remains a mystery to me. I would die a happy man if *just once* I could witness the outcome of a forced corporate buyout hinge on a best-outta-three round of "Rock, Paper, Scissors".

I must admit we later discovered that Kenny Solito could in fact — given the proper conditions — count potatoes ahead of time thereby rendering an other than random outcome. Seriously, how many times in a row can a guy *go first* without arousing suspicion? But Kenny's dead now and, being Catholic and all, I think he's probably in Limbo — so I won't go into it.

Once having determined who gets *first pick,* it naturally follows that the other team captain gets the *next two.* After that, it's one each until such time as you either have enough players or you run out of kids. Normally by that point you're down to "no counts" anyway — those kids who are pretty much just in the way regardless of the game. Usually the process is fairly cut and dried.

Situations may arise however that aren't so straightforward. Situations where you might have, say, two extra Catholics or vice versa. Sometimes the only remedy — if you still want to play at all — is for somebody to *play for the other team.*

Being selected to play for the other team is a kid's worst nightmare. Not only does being deemed expendable by your own guys destroy any self-esteem you might be harboring but it invariably means being relegated to the other team's least important position. Full time center. Permanent blocker. Positions from which a game can hardly be thrown. To one team you're not to be trusted — you may not even be made privy to a *trick* play for fear you'll telegraph it to your former teammates. Winks and nods are passed behind your back. You become paranoid. Meanwhile, to the other team — through absolutely no fault of your own — you're a traitor.

All you can really do is play a half-hearted game. Not good. Not bad — a performance guaranteeing you the same dilemma the next time a similar situation presents itself. It's a lose-lose proposition. For losers.

Catholics tend to run in *packs* so more often than not it was *they* who would have too many available players. *We* on the other hand, tended toward more individualistic, come-and-go-at-will behavior. For instance, while *we* may get called home at any time for any reason — Catholics with their more regimented life-style would typically get called home all at the same time. This makes it statistically more likely that a Catholic kid will have to change sides in the *middle* of a game. Oddly, unlike the previous scenario, this may actually work to a kid's advantage. Having already proven yourself on the *other side of the ball,* your status can actually be enhanced if it is shown that the winning team is whichever side you happen to be playing on. Altogether different stakes — often prompting even *good* players to volunteer to "bite the bullet" and switch teams. Those are the real traitors in this world.

The *up side* to this whole switching sides deal was the cultural exchange. We knew and were on better terms with some Catholics than others and that's where Jack and Jim Cassidi come in.

After some hushed (but rather heated) debate, Bobby and I settled on one last gambit. We would, at least try to, swing a deal with Jack and Jim Cassidi. For the first time in the real world my diplomatic prowess would be tested.

Leaving the relative safety of the mulberry tree, we advanced, upright and unarmed, directly toward the Catholic stronghold — continuing the ruse (minus the swagger). Leveraging our *perceived* position of superior force and manpower.

Anxiety spawned by impending doom was evident in the Cassidi brothers' eyes as we approached, such that, even as they stood up to confront us, dirt clods at the ready, they seemed dismally ill prepared for the "Alamo" fate that was surely about to befall them.

Raising both hands to form a "T" — I called "time out".

In the kids' world few things carry the weight and immediacy of a called timeout. I have actually heard "Timeout. Timeout. I think you broke my tooth" called in the middle of a fistfight. Even knowing this, Jack and Jim Cassidi hesitated momentarily but after exchanging glances and subsequent shrugs, they lowered their dirt clods. After all, they really couldn't fare any worse by stopping to listen, could they? They were living on borrowed time and they knew it. They knew we knew it and we knew they knew we knew it.

I turned facing the opposite side of the turnip field and signaled timeout to our forces — a nice touch I thought. A little more relaxed now, the Cassidi brothers waved us into their stronghold.

The Catholics fort was comprised of a semi-circular mound of grass-covered dirt, open on the back side, neat piles of dirt clods arranged at strategic points beside depressions along the wall. Five or six two-by-fours had been nailed together to form a viable table around which large flat rocks had been arranged for seats — all-in-all a fairly impressive setup.

Near the back *entrance* sat a cooler of Kool-Aid, a scattering of Dixie-Cups, and a Superman lunchbox burgeoning with peanut butter and jelly sandwiches neatly wrapped in wax paper — obviously Mom-made. These guys were living like kings and I could see why they were so happy about not being sequestered at some church camp.

They offered us each a paper cup of Kool-Aid and half a sandwich, which we accepted in the spirit of good faith and harmony, plus we were suddenly starving. Then we got down to the business at hand.

Acting as though we didn't know how outnumbered they were — I explained the proposition.

"Look, here's the deal. We have a treasure map."

That got their immediate attention and the atmosphere changed from one of anxiety to one of serious interest. I let that sink in for a minute before continuing.

"The problem is, it's gonna be hard to dig it up in the middle of a war...so we've been sent to offer you guys a deal."

"Is this a trick?" Jim asked.

"No trick."

"Cross your heart, hope to die, stick a needle in your eye?"

"Cross my heart, hope to die, stick a needle in my eye," I answered crossing my heart. Crossing one's heart means a whole lot in Catholic.

"OK, so what's the deal?"

"It's buried treasure. Can you come up with a shovel?"

The Cassidis looked at each other, "Yeah. We can get a shovel."

"Good. We've got the map — it cost me a whole bag of marbles," I lied, and continued in a more subdued tone, "Nobody even knows about it except me and Bobby — and now you guys."

Now *they* knew something *even our own guys* didn't know. They had been brought into the *inner circle*. The conference assumed a somewhat more devious quality. Rule number one of negotiating: You can't cheat an honest guy.

The Cassidis instinctively looked first over toward our fort then back over their shoulders. Deciding the coast was clear Jim said, "Go on."

"You guys get a shovel; I'll show you where to dig; we'll split the treasure — one part for me, one part for Bobby and one part for you guys."

The Cassidis didn't flinch at the split. Protocol demanded that, in a situation such as this, the loot be divvied up on a per family basis. Plus, being how it was *our* map and all, it was only fair that they should do the digging.

"What about your other guys?" Jack wanted to know.

"I'll send them all home."

"How you gonna do that?"

"Don't worry about it. I'll take care of them. No problem."

With that the Cassidi brothers' whole demeanor changed. They apparently hadn't realized I wielded so much sway over my peers.

"So, *deal?*"

"Deal."

We all shook on it like football captains at a coin toss then Jack ran off to get his old man's genuine U.S. Army entrenching tool while I ran off to "square it with the rest of our guys" and to get the map. I actually had the map on me the entire time but the better part of discretion dictated we not divulge that up front. Remember, a half-hour earlier we had no clue how well or even *if* our hastily hatched plan would work. As I look back over a career wherein I brokered many a deal — some *pro bono* and some worth literally millions of dollars — I still regard this particular one as the sweetest.

After reenacting our movements of earlier — pacing off twenty steps from the mulberry tree to the spot signified by the "X" on the map — we began digging.

The ground was extremely hard but soon Jack and Jim Cassidi got the hang of it and were making good headway. With each shovelful of dirt we expected to hear the undeniable "thunk" of metal on treasure chest.

Throughout the remainder of the morning and into the afternoon the Cassidi brothers took turns manning the shovel. At one point we stopped to rest and contemplate the map some more. Ultimately deciding whoever buried the treasure might have possessed a longer gait than any of us kids, we paced it off again — this time taking the biggest steps we could take, not

unlike a line judge stepping off a twenty yard penalty —
and started anew.

After awhile, Bobby and I opted to try our hand at
digging — sighting that the Cassidis were beginning to
wear down and needed a break. Although it was true,
they did need a break, in truth we figured maybe they
were just *unlucky*. It turns out — digging for treasure is
hard work.

We worked until nearly sunset when the Cassidis
were called home. Though Bobby and I offered to stay
and dig for as long as possible, Jack and Jim were
naturally wary of leaving us alone with the treasure,
saying they'd get clobbered if they returned home
without their old man's genuine U.S. Army entrenching
tool. They had a point, even if we didn't really believe
them. A genuine U.S. Army entrenching tool is not
something you want to leave out of your sight for a
whole night. That's definitely bad juju in anyone's
book. We agreed to pick up where we left off at eight
o'clock the following morning.

I set my alarm clock that night to wake me every
hour on the hour at which time I would sneak outside
and, using my homemade spyglass, search the night
horizon for any telltale signs of flashlights, lanterns,
what have you. We didn't really trust the Cassidi
brothers either. My guess is they did likewise. It was a
long night. Oddly enough we all showed up back at the
dig site around six o'clock in the morning.

By the end of day two we had dug no less than forty
holes. Big ones. Little ones. Deep ones. Shallow ones.
Reckoning there might have been an honest mistake in
the instructions, we even tried pacing off twenty steps
away from Casperson's Market. Then, just in case they
had inadvertently left off a zero, we paced off two

hundred steps in both directions. We tried every combination of probable and even just *possible* misrepresentations of the treasure's location...be they error induced or intentional. No good.

In the heat of the noonday sun on day three of our treasure salving operation we decided to call it quits. We'd come along too late. Obviously someone had beaten us to it. I have to say it was a sobering disappointment but...it wasn't a total wash. For one thing, we did dig up four arrowheads — one for each of us — in addition to what we believed to be a petrified shark's tooth...so that was cool.

Then too was the cultural exchange. Bobby and I learned that Catholics can be OK guys once you get to know them and I think the Cassidi brothers came away with the same sentiment toward us. We had, it turned out, unknowingly forged an alliance that would later figure into what ultimately would be the Eggless Club's greatest adventure ever.

6

Grandma's House and Wino

Where I grew up, things seldom originated locally. Unless something was homemade, there's a good chance it came from Japan or Hong Kong or even as far away as Chicago. Events didn't just occur — they too came from other places.

Guys got what was comin' to 'em. Halloween and Christmas and luck came and went. Where they came *from* or where they went *to* didn't matter. Some things were more aptly described with respect to their conveyance — things like ideas might come in a flash while other things might just hit you — having come from out of nowhere. One day us kids' ship came in. It came in the form of information. It came from Wino.

We had gone to visit my great grandmother. She lived in a big city that took a long time to get to. Long as in *you had to stop and eat just to get there* long. Oftentimes the stopping to eat part was the highlight of the trip for us kids — not this time.

Grandma had no name of her own. As far back as I can remember she had been simply "Grandma" to young and old and *really* old alike. Even the mailman called her Grandma, though I don't think he was actually blood kin — he was, after all, a whole different color. Grandma lived in a huge Victorian house (Victorian is German for "really, really creepy") surrounded by walls and vines that smelled really good to girls but nauseating to boys.

We loved going to Grandma's because Uncle Rusty lived there. He was a lot of fun and knew how to catch bees. Bees will sting you if you don't do it right. Uncle Rusty showed us both ways. Bees love nauseating vines.

We loved visiting Grandma but dreaded staying overnight. Her house creaked and groaned all night long and complaining didn't do any good. Grownups would say, "It's just the house 'settling' for the night," as if that helped. It didn't. Sure maybe to civil engineers and such but not to kids. Not only did it *not* help but, if anything, it functioned as a creepiness multiplier. That wasn't the worst part of spending the night at Grandma's.

The worst part about spending the night at Grandma's was if you wanted a drink of water — or even worse, if you had to go to the bathroom — in the middle of the night. Getting to the bathroom meant passing by a heat vent in the wall about halfway down the hallway *between* you and the bathroom. Like everything else in Grandma's house it was the *old* kind. The creepy kind. It had louvers that would suddenly pop open whenever the furnace kicked on. Once opened, *anything* could grab you. We had never seen *it* but it had hot breath and probably eyes.

Making it to the bathroom was a lot like stealing second base. First, you had to take a good lead — but not *too* good — then, when the time was *right*, make your move. Speed wasn't the only athletic requirement.

Any kid — at least any *live* kid — knows instinctively that a straight run would just leave you vulnerable to a bloody hand (or possibly a tentacle) darting out from the heat vent — tripping you up at the worst possible moment and there you'd be, lying on the floor (no doubt covered in slime) feet struggling desperately to get some bite on Grandma's highly polished hardwood floor. An easy kill. Your only redemption — if you're lucky — would be that your heart would burst from fright before you got dragged all the way *in*.

On the other hand, that the ominous louvered heat vent was so close to the floor would also prove to be its weakness. It could be defeated. A well-timed combination hurdler/broad-jumper move was the key. Naturally, there are as many approaches to this as there are kids but I preferred the "step-count" method myself.

Simply having cleared the *creepy-old-time-louvered-heat-vent-beast's* airspace, however, did not mean your problems were over. Not by a long shot. Now, you had to *stop*.

Highly polished oak hardwood floors were never designed for stopping, anymore than for starting, and *overrunning the bag* in this case meant slamming into the wall at the far end of the hallway — only to be found the next morning by horrified siblings — unconscious and half eaten.

Of course, getting to the bathroom was only half the ordeal. You still had to get back. Fortunately getting back — like most things in life with the exception of say, a urinalysis — is easier because you no longer have to pee — so there's that. Plus, if you hang out in the bathroom long enough, there's a good chance reinforcements will arrive. The obvious advantages of this are covered at length in "Kids Survival Handbook".

[See: Fifty-Fifty Chance the Monster/Beast Will Eat and/or Disembowel the Other Guy Theory — Merger Clauses 37-42 inclusive]

Living on our wits, we survived many a night at my great grandmother's house and this night proved to be no exception.

The following morning we were up and out of the house early. Don't get me wrong, we all loved spending time with Grandma — and she loved having us around — but there were *way* too many ways to get into trouble. Too many ways to die — especially in the house.

For most people, when you say "great grandmother" it congers up visions of some frail little old lady stopping every couple steps to allow the oxygen to catch up. Not my Grandma. She was big and strong — an old German grandma. She had been in wars. Wars that her side lost. Wars where she held wounded guys down while teams of Army surgeons cut off parts of their bodies. She didn't like to talk about that stuff much, at least not enough for us kids anyway, but other than that we thought she was pretty tough.

Mostly she would sit for hours or even days at a time reading from an old, beautifully handwritten German Bible. It must have weighed a hundred pounds. Besides reading her Bible, her other hobbies included cooking and cleaning. Grandma's house was absolutely immaculate. Scary clean. A museum of knick-knacks in crystal glass cabinets and plates hanging on the wall that you weren't allowed to even eat on and an old shorthaired cobby-body Chihuahua named Phoebe who hated kids. You absolutely *did not* mess around with Grandma's cool stuff. She'd know it if you did (I think Phoebe was a *fink*).

She too had lobster claws (a la my old man — no doubt from lugging around that massive Bible) along with a sixth — maybe even a seventh — sense that alerted her to stuff you were only just *beginning* to *think* about doing. Again, the prudent course of action called for getting up early and getting out of the house.

For some reason Uncle Rusty wasn't there this time. Whenever Uncle Rusty wasn't there to goof around with, we'd go see Wino. Naturally, we weren't allowed to go see Wino, at least as far as my mother was concerned, but Grandma never minded. She was really cool about stuff like that. She'd say things like, "Oh, they're out back," or, "I just saw them next door a minute ago, not to worry. Ach, Mien Gutten Himmel." Really cool.

Wino was deathly afraid of my great grandmother. I remember one occasion when Grandma's mail had been mis-delivered to Wino's house and he brought it over to her. That was the first (in fact, the only) time we ever saw Wino in a suit and tie. Wino wasn't afraid of *anything*. Wino was deathly afraid of my great grandmother.

Wino was an old, old, old black man (actually he used the term "colored" when he explained it all to us one day) who spent all day every day — and most of the night — on the wrap-around front porch of his house on the corner at the other end of Grandma's block. There he'd sit in his wheelchair drinking milk, watching traffic and waving to passers-by. Whenever anyone would stop to talk to Wino they'd always leave smiling and laughing. Wino was really cool. Sometimes he'd use words that *we* weren't allowed to use but then he'd always tell us not to go around repeating them. The only time we used *those* words was in the context of accurately recounting a particular Wino story to the guys. Usually.

We never knew what a "wino" was. We just figured it was his name. It never occurred to us that it probably wasn't his *real* name. I mean, when's the last time you walked up to some guy and asked, "What's a Fred?" or, "What's a Mister Harrison?" right? One day years later our grandmother explained about Wino.

Grandma told us how Wino had spent his life as a "steel walker". A steel walker is some guy who walks around on steel girders, at dizzying heights, tossing red-hot rivets around and catching them in buckets — a noble profession that paid reasonably well for as long as you lived. That much we already knew. In fact, for years, that's what I wanted to be — a steel walker. An incident involving a two-foot step stool would later cure me of *that* ridiculous ambition. What we didn't know was that every day Wino would fill a milk carton with wine before heading to work. One dew-slick morning it all caught up with him and now he lived in his wheelchair on the front wrap-around porch of his house on the corner.

Wino had been everywhere and done just about everything. All those years of tossing rivets around had sure enough given him a strong throwing arm. Did you know that one time he knocked an Indian Chief clean off his horse with a single stone throw from six hundred yards away?

"To be truthful," Wino would say, "it mighta' been only about five hundred yards or so — kinda' hard to tell in all that fog and all. Stopped the whole battle before it even got started. Go look it up. You won't find that battle listed nowheres. Why? Because it never happened, that's why! Stopped it before it even got started!"

Wino was right too; there's not a word about it in anything we were ever able to find.

Beyond Wino's house — across the street — an old industrial park filled with long-defunct factory buildings stood in nearly functional ruins. It looked really cool and we were antsy to check it out. Originally we had planned to only stop by and say "Hi" to Wino (maybe listen to a story or two) before sneaking over to investigate the inner workings of an abandoned machine-shop in the industrial complex. I'm sure glad we stopped to talk to Wino first.

We told Wino about our treasure map and how we'd been suckered. He just laughed and slapped his knee. I think he used to slap his knee so he wouldn't laugh too hard.

He said, "Oh yeah...you gots to watch out for the 'gotchas'. Oh yeah. Cause the gotchas'll getcha!" Then he laughed some more. "No, you boys gots to look, and you gots to listen. You gots to use your brain. That's why you gots one. If ya'll boys don't use your brain then you're just carrying around extra weight for nothin'."

It made sense. We'd never thought of it that way before. I guess that was his point. We told him we were going to start using our brain. We would never get "got" again!

Wino just smiled and said, "Mmm hmm." Wino always said, "Mmm hmm," when he didn't believe you.

We were anxious to get across the street but when Wino heard our intentions he just laughed. Of course,

Wino was always laughing, but this was an *I know something you don't know* kinda laugh.

"Oh, you boys go ahead on, but *I* sure wouldn't. Nope, you won't see me goin' anywheres *near* that place. Not me. Not no *way*. Not no *how*."

"Why not?" We wanted to know, "What's wrong with over there? It *looks* really cool."

"Oh yeah, I reckon it *looks* really cool and all...to ya'll what don't knows the 'whole' story. But, ya'll boys go ahead on. I'll just sit here and watch. Let's see, there's four of you? OK. I'll just wait here and see how many of ya'll make it back out."

"Make it back out? Whaddaya mean?"

Wino thought for a while...hesitant to say any more. Finally he said, "Well, I kinda promised I wouldn't never say nothin' because Johnny Eyeball and me...well...because we was good buddies back then. Back before it happened."

It? There's an *it?* That got our attention.

"What happened, Wino? Who's Johnny Eyeball? C'mon, you can tell *us*. Pleeeeease. C'mon."

Wino sat for a long time — no doubt reliving it in his mind — eventually deciding to let us in on it.

"Well, I guess it won't do no harm to tell you boys, us being *pals* and all. But you can't never tell Johnny Eyeball I said nothin'. You know he has *ways* to make a kid *talk*."

With a shiver and grimace Wino seemed to imply said "ways" were...not good. Still, we had to know.

"We won't. We won't ever say a word. Never ever. We promise."

Wino eased back into his chair, scruffy chin in hand.

"Whelp, Johnny — back then we just called him 'Johnny' — was real, real strong. If I recall, he used to play Quarterback for the Brooklyn Dodgers. Real strong. In fact, one time he was almost Mr. America. I think he woulda' been too — 'cause he was real big and real strong — but he stopped to lift up a school bus so's they could change a flat tire. Ya know, he didn't even make them kids get off that bus or nothin' — that's how strong he was. Well, by the time he got to that Mr. America place they had already picked some other guy. I'll just betcha though, if he hadn't stopped to help them kids he woulda' won that thing. He was real strong.

"Anyway, a couple weeks later Johnny and me, we was over there in Germany fightin' the Japs. We was whippin' 'em real good too. All the way outta' France and right up Mt. Iwo Jima...right towards Berlin. When we got up over the top of that hill I took out my binoculars and, way down at the bottom, I could see the King of the Japs — Adolf Hitler hisself. 'Course ol' Johnny didn't need no binoculars 'cause he had a 'eagle eye'. He could see everything all the way down there, clear as day.

"Whelp, we was standin' there plannin' what to do next when all of a sudden a Nazi Panzer tank came out from behind a bunch of palm trees and, just like that, Johnny and me, we was lookin' straight down the barrel of a big ol' tank gun! I think it was a thirty-eight caliber but it mighta' been bigger. I know it sure enough looked big. Next thing ya know that thing shot a tank bomb at us. Don't ya know Johnny saw that tank bomb a comin', 'cause he had a 'eagle eye', and he pushed me outta' the way just in time."

We sat listening in awe. This guy Johnny wasn't just big and strong but he had an eagle eye too. And he was a genuine war hero to boot. A sadness came over Wino.

"I guess ol' Johnny just wasn't very lucky that day. Ya see, that tank bomb missed *me* but then it went and bounced off of a big ol' rock that was just sittin' there and came back and hit Johnny right in the head. I reckon Johnny was a little lucky though 'cause he had his helmet on, so when that tank bomb blew up he was almost OK. Almost OK...but not quite OK. Don't ya know when that tank bomb blew up, a piece of it bounced off of that same rock and hit ol' Johnny right in the eye. Yes sir, knocked Johnny's eyeball plum out."

We all gasped in unison. "That's really gross."

"Let me tell you, boys, it was 'way gross'. It was the grossest. I looked up and there was Johnny — covered with blood — one eyeball hanging down to about here." Wino indicated a point about chest high then continued, "Hangin' there by a big ol' vein. A 'optical vein'. Oh yeah, it was gross alright. So gross I don't like to even think about it."

"So, what'd he do then?" We had to know.

"Then? Well, I'll tell you what he did then. Ol' Johnny he got mad. Real mad. Madder'n I ever seen *anyone*, before or since. He grabbed that ol' rock and started runnin' down that hill a yellin' and a cussin'. Them Japs was a yellin' too. They was shootin' all around him but they couldn't hit 'im. Nope, they sure couldn't and ya know he ran right up to that Hitler fella' and smashed his head clean open! And then Johnny just stood there all surrounded by those Japs."

We boys sat transfixed, all figuring that had to be it for Johnny. There's *no way* a guy could get out of that jam — we thought. "So did the Japs shoot him?"

"Nope. That's what I figured too but nope, they sure didn't. As soon as them Japs saw that King Hitler was dead they called the war 'over' and they all went home. That was it. Just like *that*," Wino snapped his fingers for effect, "the war was over. Once them Japs all went home then me and Johnny — we came home too."

"So, what happened to Johnny? Did they fix his eye?"

"Nope. Couldn't fix it. Oh, they tried alright. A whole bunch of Army doctors and Colonels and stuff. They tried real real hard too. For a whole week. But they couldn't fix it. Nope. They said 'cause Johnny ran all the way down that hill with his eyeball a hangin' out, it stretched out that optical vein so's they couldn't fix it. Oh, they could put it back in alright so's it didn't look too bad or nothing, but the problem was...if you walked up and said, 'Hey Johnny,' whelp — whenever he turned around to see who it was, you know that ol' eyeball of his would just pop right back out. It would scare the girls and stuff. Then he'd just get really really mad all over again. And believe me buddy — you do *not* wanna be the guy what said his name. Not no *way*. Not no *how*.

"Well, at first everyone started calling him Popeye and Johnny was OK with that I reckon but it turns out that name was already taken."

Wino was right. We knew that for a fact. There already was a Popeye.

"So then everyone started calling him 'Johnny Eyeball' and he didn't like that *at all*. Not one bit. In fact he hated it but...that's the name that stuck.

"After that, Johnny went to live over there in those old factory buildings where he wouldn't never have to see nobody and nobody wouldn't never have to see him."

"So do you ever see him over there?"

"Oh yeah, all the time...at first. In fact he used to come over here every once in awhile when no one else was around. Ya know, that ol' eyeball, it never bothered me none — I told you we was buddies back then. But, ya know, he just kept gettin' madder and madder and I think he started gettin' kinda crazy. Then he started to get mean. Real mean. After that he just quit comin' over at all. The last time I saw him I don't think he even knew who I was.

"So, I thought maybe if I just left him alone for awhile, maybe he'd get better — but he didn't. I think the biggest problem was those kids what *used* to live in that big green house down there," pointing to the big green house down there. "Now them kids, them kids was real mean and they used to throw rocks at that place where Johnny was a livin'. See where all them windows is busted out?"

Sure enough, all the windows in the old machine shop across the road had been busted out.

"Then, when Johnny would come out, one of them would count to three and they'd all yell 'Johnny Eyeball! Johnny Eyeball!' Of course when he'd turn to see who it was, his eyeball would pop right out. Then they'd all laugh and stick out their tongues and run back home. Ya know, I think that's the part what made him the maddest. Yep, stickin' out their tongues like that. That was the worst part."

"Those kids are really mean, huh?" We all agreed.

"Well, they *were* anyway."

We sat up straight. "*Were*? Whaddaya mean *were*?"

Wino looked at us kids. Squinting his eyes and looking kinda mean he repeated that single ominous word, "*Were*. Now, what they didn't know was...Johnny had done run outta food.

"Just a couple days later them kids did it again but this time it was different. This time when they went to run away, the littlest one, I think his name was Ernie — about your size," (pointing at me!) "he got hung up on that mess o' re-bar layin' over there."

We looked and there laying outside the machine shop was a chunk of concrete — tangled snakes of metal rod jutting out in all directions. A testament to dangerous stuff.

"What happened to him, Wino? What happened to that Ernie kid?" Chills ran up our spines.

"Nobody knows. When the other kids found out he was missing they all went back to get him but...he was gone. Nothin' left but a piece of his shirt and a hunk of bloody hair stuck to that 'ol re-bar over there. Nope, they never saw him again. Oh, they looked, alright. The police. The FBI. Everyone. But that's all they ever found. That piece of shirt and that hunk of bloody hair. They keep that stuff in a box down at the police station so's if they ever do find anything else they can go ahead and see if it matches."

Wino sighed and sank back into his chair. "So now whenever a kid goes in there...he just never comes back out again."

"So, why don't they put Johnny Eyeball in jail?" *That* we all wanted to know.

Wino just laughed. "No proof! They ain't gots no proof! Ya know, ya can't just go around puttin' a guy in jail. You needs proof. You gots to have *somethin'*. So far they ain't even found no bones or nothin'. Ya gots to have bones or *somethin'*.

"I *can* tell ya though, officer Hank told me just the other day they saw a guy over there wearin' a belt made *all outta tongues* but they never caught him. Remember now, Johnny was real fast. Plus, here's the deal...Johnny'd always see 'em comin'. What he'd do is...he'd take that hangin' out eyeball of his and tape it to stick. That way he could hide back behind somethin' and poke that stick around the corner so's *he* could see *you* but *you, you* couldn't see *him*. He'd always see *you* comin' first. Nope...you can't hardly catch nobody like that.

"But ya'll boys know what *I* think? Well, I'll tell ya what *I* think. You see that hole over there by that dumpster?"

We all looked over by the dumpster in the old abandoned industrial park of long-defunct factory buildings. There was a hole.

"Well, I'm pretty sure that wasn't there last week." Wino paused to let that sink in. "Now, you see that flat spot just past it?"

Sure enough, there, right where Wino said, a big flat spot — plain as anything.

"Well, I *know* there was a hole there just a couple days ago. So, *when ya'll boys get over there*...check it out for me, OK? I'll bet the ground right there is still real soft."

We all looked at each other wide-eyed. No way. Somehow in the course of hearing the story about

Johnny Eyeball we'd not only forgotten what we'd initially started out to do — we'd also lost any desire whatsoever to do it. We weren't *about* to sneak across that road and go *over there*. Suddenly it occurred to us...

"Uh, we gotta get back to Grandma's."

"Yeah, we gotta get back to Grandma's. She'll get real mad if we're late for breakfast."

Wino looked at his watch but before he could say anything we corrected that to, "Lunch, late for lunch." Wino continued. Apparently he hadn't heard us.

"Yep, I figure it'll only take ya'll boys a second to run *all the way over there* and check it out and if, I mean *when* you get back, we'll probably know for sure."

Then after what seemed like a long, long time — Wino let us off the hook.

"But I guess it's probably best not to go gettin' your Grandma all mad and all."

"Yeah, that's best. That's really best. We'll see you later, Wino."

Off we scurried leaving Wino on his front porch, drinking his milk and smiling. He was always smiling. We liked Wino a lot. I think Grandma liked him too.

Later when we went back to say good-bye to Wino before going home, we purposely waited until the last minute because we sure didn't want to risk being talked into going across that road — lest we be *chicken*.

It's a shame too because Wino had just started to tell us about a place "not too far" from where we lived. A place where the ground was covered with rubies and emeralds and diamonds as big as your fist — maybe even bigger — but in order to get there you had to cross over *Paradise Island*. That island used to be covered with prehistoric dinosaurs (solid black with yellow spots) but Wino said they were probably all dead. He was *pretty sure he had killed 'em all* but admitted to possibly having missed an egg or two.

"So, if ya'll boys ever go there, be real careful just in case there's a couple dinosaurs left over — ya know, it only takes *one o' them* to mess up your whole expedition."

Unfortunately, before we could pry any more information out of Wino, my old man pulled up out front and we had to go.

We only ever saw Wino once after that day but I will never forget the stories he told and the wonder he brought into our world. According to my calculations Wino will turn Three Hundred and Forty-Seven this year. Happy Birthday Wino.

7

Twist of Fate

Possibly the most influential event in my life was purely a twist of fate. I just happened to be there when Don came running in with the news.

Don had been hanging out at the bowling alley up at Berwick Plaza while his Mom sub'd for Old Lady Castle. Old Lady Castle had busted her arm beating a rug over the clothesline — at least that's what she claimed. As it happened, Old Lady Castle had suffered similar maladies on previous occasions — all coinciding with nights her team was slated to take on the formidable Berwick Dragonettes, a fact not overlooked by the Berwick Dragonettes themselves. Don's Mom was whispered to be a ringer. She wasn't — at least in the usual sense. She wasn't even as good a bowler as Old Lady Castle. On the other hand, she had a loud nasally voice that could peel carrots. Trying to concentrate on bowling, especially during one's approach, all the while knowing at any moment Don's Mom might blurt her way into the score-table chatter seemed to irritate the Berwick Dragonettes to no end. They always bowled ten to fifteen pins under their averages whenever Don's Mom was there.

It was a good deal for Don too. Usually the other ladies would slip him a buck (maybe two) as incentive to get lost for awhile so his Mom could bowl in peace. On this particular occasion they seemed to have forgotten that tradition but a couple well-timed "Mom, Mom, can I, can I"s slapped them back to reality. Their training seemed to kick in and they fumbled for purses in unison. So Don had cash.

Now, every place you go has rules. First are the "general rules" like: don't interrupt, don't wander off (a.k.a. stay where I can see you), and a host of others intended to make your folks not look like idiots. This category of rules tends to be fairly universal, the generally understood qualifiers of which are typically phrases like "Because I said so, that's why" optionally suffixed with "live with it" and such.

Then, you have what may be called the "worst case scenario" rules. These tend to be not just scary but prophetic in nature and include such gems as: "Never talk to strangers because God-only-knows-who could grab you and take you to God-only-knows-where for God-only-knows-what." Then there's: "Never take the short-cut home through the old open lot because God-only-knows-who could grab you and take you to God-only-knows-where for God-only-knows-what."

It is a known fact that any grownup can — off the top of their head — recite a tale of blood curdling horror about some kid who failed to recognize the wisdom of a "worst case scenario" rule. Although the details of these stories may vary from one grownup to the next, the common thread linking them to a single universal macabre tale seems to be that these kids were all "about your age" and "they had to use dental records to identify the body". These too were lessons taught by dead kids.

And then there are the "site specific" rules — uniquely applicable to particular places — like, for instance, the bowling alley. These rules tend to be more or less arbitrary. One of the rules at Berwick Plaza Lanes was that kids weren't allowed to hang out around the pool-hall. Here they had not only pool tables but also a bar. Here you heard words in the course of idle conversation that you normally only heard at home if, say, your uncle couldn't get a bolt loose, or if the Packers scored.

Here was where the *real big* kids hung out. Mostly they were post high school kids. They had cars. Some of them had jobs. Some of them had actually graduated from high school. Some of them should have actually graduated from high school but hadn't — the inevitable result of time wasted shooting pool. Here you'd find the products of misspent youth about whom Broadway show tunes had been written.

Here you could almost always find Stokes and Billy Marsh. It was these two guys in particular who could be held most responsible for our parents' inordinate dislike of pool. The fact that these guys were morons — and shooting pool had nothing at all to do with it — didn't seem to matter.

Stokes was stuck in the mid-1950s. White T-shirt, black leather jacket, cuffed jeans. Hair slicked back with a "waterfall". Stokes was a shop teacher's nightmare. A true classic, all the way down to his gray primered '47 Ford coupe, crammed with the latest Chevy 283 short-block engine, 4-on-the-floor with a Hurst T-bar, Crager Mags all the way around...you get the idea. It got rubber in three gears. That was important. If your car could squeal the tires in three gears then that alone qualified you to loop the Burger Boy parking lot on 'Vette night.

Stokes was a "pool shark". I learned that a pool shark is apparently someone who feigns pool-shooting incompetence until such time as there's money wagered on the game — then suddenly they're Minnesota Fats. I suppose I should point out that not too long afterwards Stokes was found stuffed upside-down in a wall locker at the Franklin County YMCA. Oddly enough, Billy Marsh was ultimately convicted and sentenced to prison for killing a guy and stuffing him upside-down in a wall locker at the Franklin County YMCA but that's another story.

The important thing for now is that while Don stood watching for his mother with one eye and watching the local thugs shooting pool with the other, he overheard Stokes tell Billy Marsh about a place called Paradise Island. It turns out, it was farther down the river than any of us little kids or even the big kids in our neighborhood had ever ventured.

"Yeah," Stokes was saying to Billy Marsh, "you go to about halfway between the Old Johnson farm and the bottom of Schwartz Hill and then just go due West for a long ways. There it is." Don listened intently. Cautiously. You did not want to get caught even making eye contact with Stokes or Billy Marsh let alone eavesdropping. While there had always been speculation as to exactly what would happen to you, the general consensus was: you'd be dead before you hit the ground.

Then, like a cat who had suddenly become aware of going too far out on a limb to get back, Don realized something was terribly wrong. Things were too quiet. He'd allowed his concentration to drift to the conversation between Stokes and Billy Marsh and away from keeping his eye out for his Mom. It was too late. His ear was on fire.

Mrs. Nettles was a *de facto* Mom. That is to say, she had no kids of her own. She had, however, been an elementary school teacher (in her day) so any time she saw a kid doing something she thought that kid ought not be doing, she would take it upon herself to snatch the kid by whatever part she could (usually by the ear — though we'd heard of worse) and march him over to wherever she thought he ought to be. There she would patiently hold him until the appropriate parent took possession, at which time she would go about her business, usually without a spoken word. Now she had Don. Worse — that would be all the information gleaned from Stokes and Billy Marsh.

8

Bill's Old Man and North

Don stood before us gasping to catch his breath, offering his still bright red ear not only as tangible proof of his encounter with Mrs. Nettles (lending overall credence to his story about the heretofore mythical Paradise Island) but also as an excuse for not having provided more detailed direction as to its whereabouts. Nevertheless, "half-way between the Old Johnson farm and the bottom of Schwartz Hill — then go due west," seemed like solid enough information to us. Moreover, it served to validate the actual presence of an island only rumored to exist at all.

In point of fact, it would prove to be but one of several key elements to the puzzle but as disparate pieces began to align and dovetail into place, a picture was beginning to emerge. We were closing in on it. We could feel it. Almost taste it. For starters — Bill knew which way was north.

You could always count on Bill knowing stuff like "which way was north" because he was part Indian. Actually he wasn't part Indian but his old man was. Actually his old man wasn't part Indian either but that's not really the point. The point is, at least where I grew up, if you knew anything about the stars, the moon, the sun, the wind, fishing, tying knots, or just about anything *out-doorsie* then folks just naturally figured you must be part Indian or something.

Bill's old man worked in a parts supply warehouse up in the north-end, packing small parts of specific types and quantities into individual product packages — boxing them up and shipping them to distributors all over the country. If you've ever stayed up all night Christmas Eve assembling a Big Wheel or a hobby horse then there's no doubt at some point your mind has gone numb and you've found yourself staring blankly at a plastic bag containing small parts of specific types and quantities — wondering, "Who puts all the parts into those bags?" The answer is: Bill's old man.

Miss Thelma worked the line next to Bill's old man. Complete with tied-back, old washerwoman red bandana, she could have doubled for Aunt Jemima. Miss Thelma sang Christian songs like "Closer Walk with Thee" and "Will the Circle be Unbroken," stuff like that, all day, every day. For years, this gnawed at Bill's old man's sanity but that has nothing to do with this particular story.

On Tuesdays and Thursdays, owing to her gospel/prayer/Bible-study commitments, Miss Thelma was especially interested in the time of day.

"Excuse me Mister Harrison." She calls Bill's old man Mister Harrison. "Do you know what time it is?"

Bill's old man would look up through the skylight, study the sun and the sky for a moment,

"Yeah, it's about, oh, 21 maybe 22 after 3."

This never failed to astound Miss Thelma. On several occasions she had remarked,

"I just don't get it. How DO you DO that?"

Bill's old man would explain rather matter-of-factly, "Well, ya know, I'm part Indian. From the time we're little babies we're taught to *be as one* with the plants and animals...to live and act in harmony with the Earth and heavens around us. Of course, if you weren't raised Indian then you could probably never *really* understand."

With a sigh, Miss Thelma would reluctantly have to accept that she wasn't raised Indian-style and therefore could probably never *really* understand. That put Mr. Harrison on a level above normal folks. On an almost mystical plane where he remained for nearly ten years until Miss Thelma figured out that every morning, before the start of his shift, Mr. Harrison would take off his wristwatch and set it up on the shelf between him and the skylight. After that, Bill's old man was "The Debil".

So, Bill's old man wasn't actually part Indian but it didn't matter and Bill had naturally inherited the gift. That was more than enough to qualify as our chief navigator/pathfinder. Whether by virtue of Bill's almost being part Indian or just by sheer providence, Bill knew which way was north. If you stood in Bill's side yard (next to the plum tree) and faced the water tower, that was north.

"Bill knew which way was north — so what?" you might ask.

Well I'll tell you, "so what." Dave's Aunt Connie — that's, "so what."

9

TomBoys

Where I grew up, girls had not yet been invented. Naturally, Moms and Aunts don't count. The obvious exception, of course, was Dave's Aunt Connie who was much younger than most aunts (only a year older than us) and for some reason wasn't too terribly difficult to look at — a haunting fact that tended to keep a guy oscillating between curiosity and revulsion. Only years later would I more fully understand the dynamics at play at the time but by then, as one might expect, age had caught up with Dave's Aunt Connie and she had ceased to be a girl.

Dave's Aunt Connie was considered a "TomBoy". Again, if you're one of those people who don't know what a TomBoy is, I won't bother to explain it here because you're an idiot.

OK, the rule with girls is: "You never, ever hit a girl, especially in the stomach." Now, this always seemed a somewhat strange restriction — not so much the "don't hit" part or even the "never, ever" bit (obviously included for emphasis) but the "...especially in the stomach," part. After all, "no hitting" means "no hitting", right? Everything else worked like that. "No running in the halls" means "no running in the halls" — "no biting" means "no biting", right? So why the

"...especially in the stomach" part? Isn't that kinda like saying, "Never, ever spit into the wind, especially on Thursdays?" Doesn't make a whole lot of sense does it?

Nevertheless, it didn't take a rocket scientist (even *they* had only recently been invented) to realize in short order that this one was not open for debate — even had I known expressions like *redundant* and *self evident*. "You never, ever hit a girl, especially in the stomach." I still don't.

Notwithstanding the well-documented cootie infestation issue (not their fault, really), the problem with girls is: *they* can hit *you* but *you...you* can't hit *them* — a highly discriminatory position accepted even in polite societies. Only recently have I traced the origin of this pathology back to the invention of the washing machine.

Sure, I'm a "new age" kinda guy and all that but — and I don't care who you are — getting beat up by a girl is still much worse than getting beat up by another guy. I know now that had I read Solzhenitsyn back then I'd have known that *while I may not be able to control the situation itself — how I react to the situation is always my choice.* Do they teach you *that* in elementary school? I think not. I'd have fared better.

Dave's Aunt Connie was different though. Dave's Aunt Connie was a TomBoy. Some would say, "she's the exception that proves the rule." I personally wouldn't say that because I have no idea what the hell that's even supposed to mean but suffice it to say: Dave's Aunt Connie was tough — never cried (when guys wouldn't have) — and her throwing arm was not half shabby. You wouldn't want her on first base (especially later on because she had too many parts that might get in the way) but she was great at — and loved to play — right field. Bear in mind, where I grew up we had no south-paws (I'm pretty sure they were drowned at birth) but if you came around late on a pitch she'd be there to chase it and had enough arm to peg you at second. ("Weren't expecting *that* were you, you Catholic bastard?!") So she had made a significant contribution to the team on several occasions. Not to mention "all time center".

The only *real* problem with Dave's Aunt Connie was that she more often than not represented the voice of sound reason. That'll keep you from ever doing anything. I mean sure, you might lose a buddy from time to time but that's why you have extra kids, right? You bury 'em and the squad moves out. You press on. Venture forth — lest you whither and die like pansies come Autumn.

But let there be no doubt, Dave's Aunt Connie was part of our club and *ipso facto* was privy to *most* of our escapades. That included our then upcoming journey of exploration — our quest to find the mythical Paradise Island — and this was one time having her in the club paid off. It paid off because Bill knew which way was north.

The important thing about Bill knowing which way was north was: Dave's Aunt Connie was able to take that seemingly meager snippet of information and by applying steely logic — coupled with an understanding of celestial mechanics beyond her years — determine the precise direction of due west.

"Oh, it's easy, look." Dave's Aunt Connie stood in the middle of our clubhouse, right hand on hip, left arm extended straight out in the general direction of the water tower, and said, "Never... Eat... Slimy...

Worms," executing a *right face* with each pronouncement.

She must have recognized our lack of cognizance (I for one, remember thinking, "*all* worms are slimy aren't they?") so Dave's Aunt Connie repeated the demonstration — this time replacing the original verbiage with "North... East... South... West."

Now we got it. Now we understood.

North. East. South. West. Never. Eat. Slimy. Worms. Cool.

Of course, any *guy* would have left it at that, right? But nooo, not Dave's Aunt Connie. Clearly her abnormal DNA took possession of her spirit and she quickly repeated the entire sequence. "Never Eat Slimy Worms North East South West." Spinning. Spinning with that maniacal girlie smirk that guys have come to loathe on a primitive level — finishing in an "all knowing" smile. God help us all.

Nevertheless, we all have our faults (Craig used to slobber a lot) and on the whole, Dave's Aunt Connie was OK. Plus, armed with unshakable scientific fact, we reckoned finding Paradise Island would be no problem or — at least — do-able. After all, we used to go out to Alum Creek all the time.

We weren't allowed anywhere near Alum Creek and getting caught meant a beating for sure. The merest mention of Alum Creek never failed to elicit yet another grisly "worst case scenario" tale. This one typically involving a kid "about your age" although, sometimes the kid is even older — the clear implication being, 'if it happened to *him* and he was even older, then you wouldn't have a prayer' — who "dove in, and never came up." Only after days of "dragging the river" (a task invariably charged to some guys they called the "county") would they find the body — snagged on re-bar or on an old Studebaker.

Having revisited Alum Creek in years since, I think there just might be some substance to this one.

Still...you never forget the adventure. The thrill of going to a place where perhaps no one has ever been. El Dorado. Northwest Passage. A Lost World unto itself. Not like going on a trip in the car or something — but a real adventure. This...this is better. The stuff from which legends are forged and about which classic books are written.

Paradise Island beckoned.

10

Islands In General

Frankly, we were all somewhat anxious about the whole idea. I for one had only ever been to an island once in my entire life and it wasn't really much fun. Dave figured the story warranted repeating and asked me to refresh everyone's memory...

My Uncle Pete had a boat. Actually, it wasn't his boat — rather he'd borrowed a boat from a work buddy of his down on the loading docks at the local Westinghouse distribution center. Uncle Pete got together with my old man and they decided to go fishing the following morning in Uncle Pete's borrowed boat. If I recall, the boat was only about fourteen feet long — aluminum with a small outboard motor that seemed adequate to push it around but that's probably about all.

I had found a paper carton of earthworms in the fridge and when I asked what they were for I was told to not say anything about it — *quid pro quo* I could go along. Evidently the plan had not yet gotten Mom's and Aunt Freida's blessing. My old man could have just said he liked having worms around and I would have been

OK with that but getting to go along was even better. I was excited.

Of course, the cat was out of the bag once the womenfolk got home and saw the boat hitched to my old man's car. The guys reminded their wives that they had been planning the fishing excursion for weeks — finding it hard to believe girls could forget such an important event. In truth, neither Uncle Pete nor my old man had said a word about it because they had only just decided the night before. Even then it was iffy — dependant on whether or not Uncle Pete could borrow the boat; if the boat had current registration numbers; if the trailer tires held air; and a host of other considerations.

In fact: the registration was two weeks past expiration (they figured there was probably a "grace period" on that); the tires were cracked with age and pretty badly dry-rotted; and the trailer squeaked and made other strange metallic noises when cornering. The left turn signal didn't work and the tag light was burned out but in those days you signaled a turn by sticking your arm out the window and, besides, who cares about a tag light? The planned agenda didn't call for driving at night anyway. At least the license plate was still valid and the brake lights were in working order — that's really all you need. All in all, the rig was considered "good to go".

The women of course didn't fall for the old "you knew all about it" scheme but they didn't let it show. Getting the men out of the house for a whole day would give them the opportunity to hang out together — not to mention a good excuse to go out and spend lots and lots of money. My old man and Uncle Pete had already factored that into the overall cost of the outing. So the mission was a "go".

That night, the guys made sure the women were in the kitchen making coffee when the news (more specifically, the weather) came on the television. They already knew the prediction called for rain and stormy conditions all day. I learned at an early age that you never let girls know about rain and stormy conditions if you plan on going anywhere — no good can possibly come of it.

The following morning came early and, as predicted, was rainy and dismal. What I hadn't really figured on was the *reason* it was so rainy and dismal. It was rainy and dismal because rain and dismal are typically preceded by a cold front and this time was no exception. It had been drizzling all night but Uncle Pete said as the sun came up it would all "burn off". It didn't. Still, by the time we'd loaded the fishing gear and a cooler filled with sodas and beer into the boat, the car had warmed up. It felt toasty when we piled in and got on the road. The trip had officially started and spirits were high.

We were heading to a place called Hoover Reservoir. It had nothing to do with Hoover Dam — that reservoir is called Lake Mead; go figure. It was quite a ways from our house and about an hour into the trip we pulled into a little known greasy spoon called Deep River Jim's Bait'n'Breakfast for some bacon and eggs and because both my old man and Uncle Pete were getting somewhat concerned about the trailer. The strange noises had gotten stranger and Dad said it was starting to "wander". It couldn't hurt to stop and check it out. Plus, with a little luck, the weather might clear while we were dining. It didn't. While we waited for our food to cook, Uncle Pete went out to the parking lot and inspected the trailer. He came back into the restaurant saying the axle "felt kinda hot but it ought to make it". It didn't.

About five miles out from Deep River Jim's Bait'n'Breakfast the trailer began shrieking like a banshee. With sparks shooting out in all directions and plumes of blue-gray smoke trailing from below the starboard gunwale slightly aft of amidships, Dad pulled over onto the shoulder at the first available flat spot and stopped. "Plunk." The passenger-side trailer wheel fell completely off. I was horrified. Uncle Pete and my old man agreed we were lucky the wheel had stayed on until we stopped.

Now what? I sat in the car while my old man and Uncle Pete, garbed now in ponchos, surveyed the situation. The drizzle had turned to a steady sprinkle and watching through the rear windshield I could see Uncle Pete emerge from beneath the trailer, shaking his head. It didn't look good. Not only that, he'd burned the heck out of his hand when he absentmindedly grabbed the hot axle.

After a few minutes and some more head shaking they both climbed back into the car. Having seen all there was to see outside, what they needed to decide could just as easily be discussed out of the rain. Besides, it was about time for a beer. It didn't take a lot of debate (after all, they had been kids once too) to determine that Uncle Pete had borrowed the boat — it was his responsibility. Uncle Pete could do the walking. Fair is fair. We'd been driving along a heavily wooded stretch of country road but Dad had noticed a gas station about a mile or so back — so Uncle Pete started back down the road in the direction whence we'd come.

Uncle Pete wasn't yet out of our sight when a Jeep pulled over next to him. It was (as I would soon find out) Park Ranger McGrady on his way to the main campground a few miles farther up the road. Ranger McGrady and my uncle talked for a minute before Uncle Pete climbed into the Jeep and they returned to where we were. They pulled up, parking behind the boat, and got out. My old man joined them and together they inspected the damage once more. Ranger McGrady stood up, studying something he held in his hand. Up close he looked and sounded like Johnny Cash.

"Right here's the problem," he admonished, holding a rusty, fried bearing housing. "These bearings haven't been greased in years! What're you doing using a trailer like this? Couldn't you hear it?" Looking down his sharp angular nose at my old man and Uncle Pete, it was easy to see Park Ranger McGrady didn't like guys who neglected their outdoor gear. He obviously came from a long line of men who didn't like guys who neglected their outdoor gear.

Uncle Pete said, "I just borrowed it yesterday." Ranger McGrady didn't believe him.

"If you want I can call Jim, he'll fix it."

"That'd be great. I really appreciate it." Uncle Pete smiled his friendliest smile.

Ranger McGrady didn't smile back. Still shaking his head, he walked over to his Jeep, leaned in through the window and, after flipping a switch or two, spoke into a handheld mike...

"Yeah, Jim, you there?"

"I'm here."

"I guess I owe you five bucks. I'm standin' here looking at 'em."

"Axle?"

"Yep."

"I'll be there in a minute, (Earl, boy you get your butt over here we're...)."

The radio went silent and Ranger McGrady hung the mike on its hook. Getting back into his Jeep and pulling up alongside us, Park Ranger McGrady leaned across his seat rolling down the passenger window...

"Jim'll fix you up."

Dad and Uncle Pete both tried to get in a "Thank You" but Ranger McGrady was already pulling away, rolling his window back up. They felt really, really stupid. Me too, though I wasn't quite sure *why.*

Before long a '46 Chevy pick-up pulled up behind us. Hand-painted on the side door were the words *Deep River Jim — Odd Jobs — Reasonable Rates.* Jim and his boy, Earl, got out and walked up to the trailer. Not bothering to go around to the side, Jim just leaned over to his right far enough to see the axle stub sticking out from the trailer then said, "Well boy, whataya waitin' for?"

Pulling a handful of wrenches from the leg pockets of his coveralls and tossing them on the ground, Earl went back to the pick-up, returning with a jack and a cinder block. He jacked up the trailer on one side, blocked it up then jacked up the other side. Crawling underneath, he slacked off the "U" bolts holding the axle to the frame and with a swift kick sent the axle and remaining wheel flying out the driver's side of the trailer and onto the road. The whole works teetered precariously — threatening to collapse on Jim's boy Earl at any moment — but it didn't. Jim, on the other hand, didn't flinch. He just stood there with his foot up on the guardrail, smoking a cigarette and staring off into the woods.

Jim's boy Earl picked up the axle and wheel combination from the road and together with the wheel that had previously fallen off, tossed them into the back of *Odd Jobs* before climbing into the passenger side to wait.

Deep River Jim flipped his butt off into the woods and hopped in the driver's side. As he backed around, making a three point turn, Jim said something to his boy Earl who, rolling down his window, said, "Paw says we'll be right back." Rolling his window back up, they pulled away — heading back in the direction whence they had come. The whole procedure, start to finish, took about six minutes and nineteen seconds.

Dad and Uncle Pete stood there just looking at each other. What could you say? What *was* there to say? So...we waited.

Sure enough, within the hour Deep River Jim and his boy Earl were back — axle welded and ground back to almost new. Without a word being spoken Jim stood with his foot up on the guard rail smoking a cigarette while his boy Earl reversed the previous procedure and within ten minutes the axle was back in place — the trailer again resting happily on its own two wheels. Jim's boy Earl made it look not much different than changing the back wheel on a tricycle.

Deep River Jim walked over to my Uncle Pete saying, "That oughta get you goin'. Don't know if I'd go towin' her all the way to Florida but she'd probably make it to Kentucky and back." We believed him too.

"I really appreciate the work. So...what are the damages? Uncle Pete was bracing himself for the worst.

"Whelp, let's see now...that's two wheel bearings at a buck and a half each, so that's three bucks right there, and the labor, now that's a different story. The labor's gonna run you ten bucks even, so that's thirteen dollars altogether."

We couldn't believe it, especially Uncle Pete, as he pulled out his wallet, gave Deep River Jim a ten and a five and told him to keep the change.

Jim nodded, "Much obliged."

My old man even dug out a five dollar bill and handed it to Jim's boy Earl. Earl just looked at his Paw. Deep River Jim said, "Go ahead, take it boy," and Earl took it. Grinning from ear to ear, he stuffed it in the top button-down pocket of his coveralls, "Much obliged, Mister." That kid was a *find*.

Jim's boy Earl packed up the jack and wrenches then, having raked in eighteen bucks in a little more than an hour, they drove away happy. Dad was happy. Uncle Pete was happy. Even I was happy, though I'm not really sure why. I guess country folk just naturally have a way of making people happy.

It was barely nine o'clock in the morning and we had already driven a long way, eaten breakfast, broken down and gotten back on the road. I'd learned that you never know what kind of people you're going to meet on the road. Deep River Jim's boy, Earl, was amazing. It just goes to show you what even a young lad can accomplish when he knows what he's doing. The flip-side of course is when people don't know what they're doing.

Neither Uncle Pete nor my old man is part Indian. That is to say, neither of them should probably ever go near a floating vessel of any sort — especially as the skipper.

We eventually arrived at my old man's and his brother's favorite boat ramp located at the northernmost point of the reservoir. I don't know exactly what was so great about that particular boat ramp that made it worth the extra forty-five minute drive but that's where they always insisted on *putting in.* I believe the thinking is: the farther from our house — the wilder the country. That other folks lived at the north end didn't seem to factor into the logic. That is, what was remote to us wasn't at all remote to them. My guess is, those game-fishermen came to *our* end of the reservoir for the same reason — in search of wild country.

Hoover reservoir is huge. In one direction you can't even see the far shore. On this particular day you could barely see a hundred yards through the drizzle that had turned into a sprinkle that had turned into out and out rain. It had been cold when we left our house. Now the sun was warming things at about the same rate the temperature was dropping — so it was pretty much a wash. Not really *that* cold but a little too cold to be wet. We would get wetter.

After successfully slipping the boat into the water and pulling it alongside the dock, we climbed aboard. Pumping the rubber bulb on the fuel tank and pulling the starter cord five or six times — the motor sputtered to life. Before long it seemed to warm up and run well enough, at least for a single cylinder two-stroke burning last year's gasoline. Still, it was probably a little too small for the three of us, even in that wee boat. It was definitely inadequate for the weather conditions that day but — while we wouldn't be throwing a rooster tail — it sure beat rowing and that little eggbeater did manage to push us along in the right direction. At least at first.

The following are some fundamental concepts one should keep in mind when dealing with bodies of water: If you're snorkeling — snorkel up current from the boat. If you're just out "cruising a river" — cruise upstream. If you're motor boating on a reservoir — motor upwind. The reasoning is, if something does go awry then you'll at least drift in the direction toward where you ultimately want to end up — typically back where you started. Leave the other stuff to those salty sea captain types who are duty-bound to navigate a given course as part of their job. The fact is — boats don't have brakes.

Apparently all old guys think the big fish are in the middle of the lake. In reality that's seldom the case. The sun only penetrates effectively to a certain depth — depending on the clarity of the water along with how brightly and how directly the sun is shining on the water's surface. Of course a lot of this has to do with latitude, time of year, etcetera. These factors combine to determine the types and quantities of plant life, if any, that will occur and thrive in one spot versus another.

Basically: where there's plant life, there are little fish. Where there are little fish, you'll have big fish coming to eat them. Even bigger fish will come to eat them, and so on. It's all pretty straight forward really, if you're a fish. If you're not a fish then you might do what we did — head straight downwind to the middle of the lake.

Shutting off the motor, we drifted for a couple hours — maybe longer. As the rain increased, it became more and more difficult to distinguish the shoreline. Still, we were having a good time fishing. I had plenty of sodas and the big guys had plenty of beer. I have to admit we weren't actually pulling any fish onboard but like Uncle Pete said, "That's why they call it *fishing* instead of *catching*." In fact, we were having a great time.

Dad and Uncle Pete were telling stories I'd never heard before, some of which I probably wasn't supposed to hear. Stories of things they'd done back when they were in school. Trouble they'd gotten into by doing stupid stuff when they were kids — told to me I'm sure, in hopes that I'd never repeat their mistakes.

The afternoon seemed to pass in no time. We figured we must be near the middle of the reservoir because now there was no land to be seen in any direction. The wind was starting to pick up too. The sun was fading, losing the battle with the dropping temperature. With the beer better than half gone I doubt Uncle Pete and my old man were feeling the cold as much as I was. According to Dad's wristwatch the time had come to at least start thinking about packing it in. The sun would be setting soon. Starting the motor and turning dead into the wind chilled things off even more.

As the wind increased so too did the waves. Hardly noticeable at first, now they were starting to come at us in, well, waves. What we didn't know was, what passed for the Weather Bureau in those days had been issuing tornado warnings for the better part of the afternoon. Not like nowadays — with Doppler radar and *real-time* satellite surveillance systems monitoring tornadic weather anomalies and such — in those days they'd issue a tornado warning when, and only when, someone actually *saw* a tornado and lived to tell about it. What we were in was rapidly becoming a storm — with night falling on a choppy sea of whitecaps.

Leaning closer to be heard above the din of angry weather, Uncle Pete yelled to my old man, "I don't know if we're actually getting anywhere against this wind. I don't think this motor is big enough."

Dad had been thinking the same thing but didn't want to say it. I think I would have felt better not knowing. With no land in sight and no point of reference, it was impossible to tell if we were making way or not. Normally that wouldn't be a problem, I mean, it's a lake, right? You're bound to wash up somewhere, right? But if we were blowing downwind faster than we were motoring upwind then we had a real problem. We wouldn't wash up to the edge of a lake — we'd wash up to a dam!

So, exactly what happens when you wash up to a dam in the middle of a storm? The thought of dropping off the edge of the world didn't appeal to any of us. Uncle Pete shook the fuel tank — we were getting low. Putting their heads together, our two Captains decided the prudent thing to do would be to go either right or left. Anything but dead into the wind and certainly not downwind. Of course, all of this assumed the wind hadn't shifted.

We turned to the right (starboard in boat-speak) but that brought the seas broadside — threatening to swamp us — not good. My old man had cut the tops out of some beer cans which we were all using to bail but we were losing ground. There's no way we'd be able to keep up and at this rate she'd go down quicker than we could keep her afloat. We turned back into the seas. Now we'd rise up each wave only to slam the bow back down after the wave passed beneath. We were still shipping water but we were shipping less water and, with non-stop bailing, should be able to at least keep up with it. We ended up splitting the difference, adjusting course to take the seas off our port bow. That seemed to be the best overall strategy. It was dryer than the other headings and didn't threaten to capsize us but it did tend to twist the boat with each wave — making for a pretty rough ride. Nevertheless, I recall being very impressed by the seaworthiness of the little aluminum vessel. With any luck we'd be able to reach the side of the lake before we'd reach the dam. That's when the motor stopped.

Dad and Uncle Pete took shifts yanking the starter cord to no avail. We still had fuel but it just would not start. Except for the occasional sputter — just enough to convince them to keep yanking — that was it. We were officially adrift.

It wasn't much but, taking turns cranking the motor and manning our single oar, Dad and Uncle Pete were at least able to keep our little boat pointed into the wind and heavy seas. Most of the time anyway. Every once in awhile we'd end up spinning completely around — at one point threatening to flounder — before somehow managing to get her headed back up again just in time. Now it was dark out. About as dark as it can get as a matter of fact. I think I would have been a lot more scared if I hadn't been so busy bailing. Still, we knew every minute spent drifting was taking us that much closer to the *edge*.

That's when I noticed Dad and Uncle Pete had stopped what they were doing and were staring into the darkness off the stern, straining to hear. A moment later I could hear it. The sound of waves breaking. Not

Waikiki Pounders or anything but definitely surf — each wave pushing us closer and closer to whatever was back there. Suddenly the boat shuddered, let out a horrendous metal-on-stone shriek and pivoted 180 degrees. (I remember thinking, "Arrgg! We be hard aground upon a snag!") Uncle Pete instinctively grabbed hold of the carrying handle and tilted the motor forward just as the next wave (the biggest one so far) lifted us up and forward a long ways and...deposited us upon land. Immediately hopping out of the boat, Dad and Uncle Pete greatly reduced ballast and, with the two of them lifting and pulling, the next wave swept me and the lightweight aluminum craft another thirty feet or so inland — setting us down gently in a patch of long grass at the base of a stand of pine trees. Then the wave receded. Just like that, we had been torn from the clutches of Davy Jones and granted the sanctuary of land. Not *dry* land, mind you, but land nonetheless. *Terra firma.*

My old man knew exactly where we were too. It was, in fact, a tiny island — one of only a couple tiny islands way up at the north end of the reservoir — probably not more than half a mile from the car. It turns out the wind *had* shifted. The engine flaking out is probably the one thing that saved us from God only knows what alternative fate. My old man was just unlucky enough to have his *good* luck seem like *great* luck.

Still, it wasn't over yet. It was windy and freezing. Luckily, Uncle Pete had been a Cub Scout for a couple weeks as a youth and knew exactly what to do. Under his guidance we emptied the boat, dragged it a little farther inland — just for good measure — and flipped it over. Finding a forked branch and snapping off the two branches just above the crotch, Dad used it to prop up one side of the boat. Having the boat to block the wind and provide shelter from the rain helped immensely. Sure, we might freeze to *death* but at least we wouldn't freeze *solid*. Our good fortune didn't stop there.

We'd found a Coleman lantern stashed away in the small cubbyhole in the bow of the boat and with nearly a full tank of fuel it promised (if used responsibly) to last probably all night. With it we were able to scrounge a handful of firewood — mostly chunks of discarded two-by-fours, one-by-twos and the like. Of course, everything was wet but mostly just on one side. With his pocketknife and using a rock for a hammer, Uncle Pete was able to split the dry half from the rest. The wet parts we arranged in a circle — Lincoln Log style — so they could be drying while the campfire burned in the middle. With the help of an old Life magazine — also from the bow of the boat — and a little gasoline from the outboard tank, we soon had a fire started, albeit a small one.

Having life preservers to sit on (yeah, they were wet but not as wet as the ground) and ponchos to huddle under, it wasn't really all that bad. The lantern helped. Not only did it add a touch of civility to the situation but also provided as much heat as our somewhat pitiful campfire. Too much heat as it turned out.

Some time in the wee hours of the morning the sky had completely cleared. It was cold out, the air was crisp, and the moon was full and shining bright. I had to go pee. My old man did too — I think those beers were taking their toll. Frankly, I didn't want to go alone because: the sky had completely cleared, it was cold out, the air was crisp, and the moon was full and shining bright — I think we all know what can happen on nights like that. So off we went to find a good tree. Uncle Pete took advantage of our absence by draping his poncho over his shoulders and hunching directly over the Coleman lantern, absorbing the rejuvenating heat.

I didn't think we were gone that long but when we returned, Uncle Pete looked up, white as a sheet. He started to say something...then toppled over like a sack of potatoes. I thought he was playing some kind of trick on us but Dad knew better.

He rolled Uncle Pete over onto his back and started smacking him, "Come on now Pete, don't you be dead! Dammit, you hear me? Don't you be dead!"

That's when I realized what had happened. I'd seen it before, in countless movies. Something had drained his blood! Uncle Pete had dropped his guard and, just like that — he'd been got. This was bad. If we lost Uncle Pete we'd be down to just the two of us, not good. I scanned the area in all directions but couldn't see anything. Whatever it was didn't leave a trace — not even slime. It must have come from the sea. Uncle Pete's pocketknife lay on the ground next to the campfire. Obviously, he'd tried to fend off the blood-beast but it had overpowered him. It must have happened quickly — the poor guy didn't even have time to open the knife. I grabbed the knife.

My old man smacked his brother a couple more times and Uncle Pete slowly, very slowly, started to come around.

"Pete, man don't you be doin' that now, dammit!"

Uncle Pete sat up, rubbing his head, "What happened?"

Just as I thought, the creature had sucked out his brain! Uncle Pete was rubbing the back of his neck — that's usually where they attach themselves. I was going to try to move his hand but Dad had already touched him and there was really no sense in contaminating both of us. That's not good.

"What do you mean 'what happened', you're an idiot, that's what happened!"

My old man was mad. I thought he was going to beat his brother up — that's how mad he was. He kicked a rock and, feeling better, came back over. Once again we all huddled up under the boat, on the tiny island, way up in the northern end of Hoover reservoir.

Then Dad punched Uncle Pete in the arm, "Dammit."

My old man reached into the cooler and handed me a soda then pulled out a beer for Uncle Pete and acted like was going to throw it at him but handed it to him instead. Then he got a beer for himself.

After that, they explained to me about carbon monoxide but I wasn't buying it. Can't see it? Can't even *smell* it? Yeah, right. Just what you'd expect to hear from a couple guys already starting to morph.

So there we sat, except for a couple short forays up into the trees in search of more firewood, waiting for sunrise. I didn't huddle up with those guys anymore. I just kept my distance. Dad said, "You're going to freeze your butt off," but I said I wasn't cold. I wasn't, I was just shivering. They actually dozed off for a while. At least they *looked* like it — it was hard to tell for sure. A couple times I tossed a pebble over by them to see if they'd inadvertently expose a reptilian eye but they didn't. Oh, they were good. I scooted to where I could keep a close eye on both the lake and them. With Uncle Pete's knife secreted under my poncho I was as ready as I'd ever be for an attack from any direction as I sat there banking on the beast only venturing out to feed...once a night.

Several hundred years later the sun peeked up over the horizon. It felt good. Good and warm. And safe — not because the sun was up but because the full moon was down. I figured I wouldn't have anything to worry about until nightfall.

Things look different in the daytime. In the bright sunshine the island was actually smaller than the night before. Scouring the rocky beach Uncle Pete found a fairly good stack of dried branches along with assorted flotsam and this time built an impressive campfire. As the sun rose higher we didn't really need the fire but it just seemed like the thing to do and it did take what little chill there was out of the air as we began gathering our gear and breaking camp.

Flipping the boat back over and toting it to the water's edge, we mounted the outboard back on the transom (just in case it should start) and loaded up all of our stuff. After that we set the boat in the water up to the bow. We'd found one of those long triangular flat stakes that surveyors stick in the ground to mark their sightings and figured it would have to suffice as a better-than-nothing second oar. That and one real oar would serve as our power plant. I was assigned to keep the boat from drifting away while Dad and Uncle Pete doused the campfire with beer cans of lake water then, satisfied we'd left nothing behind, we bid farewell to our beneficent little island and shoved off.

It didn't take long to round the lee side of the island but the moment we did we got the full force of the wind blowing — just like the day before — from the north. Paddling against it was not going to be easy.

That's when we noticed the Marine Patrol vessel heading directly for us. Beyond it, off in the distance, we could see not just Dad's car but Uncle Pete's car too. Between them stood two people looking out to sea. Apparently, sometime after midnight the women had freaked out and notified the "authorities". Never tell girls where you're going — at least if you want to avoid this kind of scene. It gets better.

As the Marine Patrol vessel drew closer we could clearly see, standing next to the skipper, Park Ranger McGrady. He wasn't the least bit surprised to see us. Whatever he leaned over and said to the skipper must have been funny because the boat swerved a couple times before correcting course. They pulled alongside our boat, giving us *just* enough wash to *not* swamp us.

The skipper tweaked the throttle — holding the vessel dead still in the water — as Ranger McGrady stood towering overhead, looking down on us from his vantage point along the port gunwale. Those boats are really big up close.

"You know, if it wasn't for the kid I'd leave your butts out here."

He let that *sink in*. Ranger McGrady still looked like Johnny Cash...but on a boat.

"OK. Toss me a rope."

Well, we didn't have a rope. The skipper turned away. He *had* to. Even from behind, you could still tell he was grinning like there was no tomorrow as he busied himself digging through a box no doubt containing rope. Deftly moving aft, he made the rope fast to a stern cleat, handed Ranger McGrady the bitter end and went back to smiling and manning the helm.

Ranger McGrady threw the rope at Uncle Pete who promptly tied it to the bow eye with a Granny knot. Rolling his eyes, Ranger McGrady moved inboard as slowly and smoothly the huge Marine Patrol vessel rotated to a heading coinciding with the boat ramp. The rope gave up its slack and we were under tow.

I half expected the skipper to throttle all the way up but he didn't. Upon reflection I don't think he was ever laughing at *us* at all. I think he figured we were just pathetic. It was Johnny Cash having to *deal* with idiots like us that was funny and I had the feeling the skipper wanted the trip to *last*.

As we approached the dock the women folk were there to greet us. They were happy, angry, sad, frustrated, and had been worried sick and crying for hours. They were having a hard time coping. As soon as we made port Mom said, "We'll see *you* at home!" and with that they piled into Uncle Pete's car and drove off — not even a backward glance.

Dad and Uncle Pete tried to look as salty as possible gathering the boat onto the trailer and pulling it out of the water. They didn't look the least bit salty. Meanwhile, the skipper busied himself studying the boat and its contents and writing things down on an official looking pad sandwiched in a leather binder made especially for official looking pads. No "throwable floatation device". No Class A/B fire extinguisher. No anchor. The list went on. Expired numbers (it turns out Ohio has no grace period on boat registration). He even made note of a minor being aboard the unsafe vessel and the open beer cans.

After checking the time on his watch and adding it to the official looking pad the skipper tore the citation from the book and handed it to my old man who handed it to Uncle Pete. Uncle Pete stood there reading it with Dad looking over his shoulder to read it too. Apparently all of those violations were a really big deal. Special Board of Inquiry. The opportunity to appeal decisions. Something about a Magistrate.

The skipper said, "You'll be hearing from us. In the meantime, if it were me, I'd get as much of that corrected as I could."

Then after a quick (what can only be described as) *girly smirk* to Park Ranger McGrady, the skipper boarded his vessel and powered back out into the reservoir.

Once the skipper had left, Ranger McGrady pulled my old man and Uncle Pete off to the side. He picked the Notice of Maritime Violation(s) from Uncle Pete's hand, folded it and stuck it into his badge pocket.

"I'll just keep this in my desk for now but," he looked real mean and said, "I don't want to ever see you boys back at my lake again — because I *will* remember it's in there."

Dad and Uncle Pete both promised they wouldn't dream of ever coming back to Park Ranger McGrady's lake again.

"You just remember what I said. Now git before I change my mind."

By the time Johnny Cash had walked across the parking lot and climbed into his Jeep, we had already got.

Neither Uncle Pete nor my old man ever went back to Park Ranger McGrady's lake again. Lately I've been thinking about going back but it's only been fifty-some years. I'm thinking in another twenty or so, the heat will have blown over.

While that may have been my one and only *first-hand* experience being on an island, one thing was certain: if we were planning on going to an island — we obviously needed to talk *logistics*.

11

Logistics

Any journey of consequence requires planning. How long will it reasonably take to get there and back? How about unreasonably? There are a lot of "what ifs". How much of *this* and how much of *that* might you need — both minimum and worst case. Logistics.

The need for such basics as food and water are obvious even to boys. It's the actual amounts we tend to underestimate. That's because boys generally live in the moment so if I'm not hungry now then it's safe to assume I'll never be hungry again. Plus, if it comes right down to it "I can always hunt and fish for food and otherwise survive on my wits" is the typical male mindset.

Boys do tend to carry enough water but only because canteens are cool — although an empty canteen is just about as cool as a full one, especially if slung from the proper web gear. There's really no reason to lug around a heavy canteen if there are known water sources along the way — so long as you don't mind drinking dirty, critter-infested water. We didn't.

The truth is, drinking dirty water is probably one of the healthiest things a boy can do. Those of us kids who grew up in my neighborhood had enough antibodies in our systems that any one of us could have meandered through a Bubonic plague ward and the only ones who'd need be concerned would be the Bubons — and possibly Charles.

Charles was a new kid. Actually, Charles was a perpetual new kid. He was an Air Force brat. About the time his family would get settled, his old man would get reassigned to another airbase so Charles was one of those kids who you knew for awhile, then one day he was gone, never to be seen or heard from again. That's probably for the best.

Charles was a weird kid. For one thing he insisted (as did his folks) on being called Charles. Not Charley or Chuck but Charles — even when his parents weren't around. So Charles arrived in our neighborhood with four or five strikes against him already.

Charles was one of those guys who were always getting hurt. Not just cuts and scrapes and bruises — typical boy stuff — but bad hurt. The *everyone gets in trouble because this idiot can't keep from clobbering himself* kinda hurt. If scars are truly evidence of lessons learned then Charles was the most educated guy I have ever known.

If we played mumbly-peg Charles would end up with a knife stuck in his foot. If you're going to flinch then any *normal* kid would move *away* from ground zero. Not Charles. Normal kids also know better than to tell their parents. Not Charles. So *we'd* get a beating for having Bobby's old man's favorite pocketknife while the village idiot ends up in the emergency room getting a tetanus shot. You'd think he'd know better after that but — not Charles.

Not long after that incident (nearly everything Charles had a hand in was ultimately deemed an "incident") Charles determined to show-off his mechanical aptitude by demonstrating how to reload his mother's stapler. As you might already have guessed, upon closing the device he managed to shoot the first staple into his finger.

Later, after covertly returning the stapler to its proper place in his mother's home office, Charles was caught sneaking back out of the room and when his mother asked about his bloodstained hand — he choked. He told his mother he had been bitten by a snake. You'd think he'd pulled a head out of a bag. Never, ever tell a girl you've been snake-bit.

Still, a quick thinking kid, having recognized the flaw in his story, could have gotten out of it — not Charles. As the interrogation intensified, Charles could simply have said it was, say, a garter snake. But not Charles. Revealing nothing short of a criminal lack of forethought, Charles said the worst possible thing. He said he didn't know *what* kind of snake it was. His mother totally freaked out.

Before you know it, Charles and his mother were piled into a Chevy wagon, racing at break-neck speed toward the medical facility at Lockbourne Air Force Base. At that point, Charles couldn't come clean. He was in too deep to get out.

Charles spent the rest of that day and well into the night getting poked with needles, some to put stuff *in* — some to suck blood *out*. Then, when he'd least expect it, other folks would show up to painfully scrape skin samples into Petri dishes and otherwise do all the things medical personnel are bound to do when confronted with puncture wounds of unknown reptilian origin coupled with inconclusive test results.

Eventually it was determined, in classic military fashion, that if the snake had been venomous then Charles "would have been dead by now" and Charles was returned home in the wee hours of the morning, exhausted, covered in bandages and looking very pale from the ordeal — the fruits of pain and suffering borne of sheer stupidity.

On another occasion we had all snuck off to Alum Creek to do some fishing. Naturally, Charles wasn't satisfied with *our* favorite fishing hole and decided to try his luck farther upstream. Somehow he managed to trip over his fishing pole and hook his own arm. As if that wasn't bad enough, he'd done it in such a way as to end up lying on his back with the pole wedged between two rocks. Subsequent efforts to get up resulted in the pole flexing — tensioning the line and hooking him even deeper. In effect he was stuck. Lying there...stuck on his own fishing pole.

You don't even want to admit knowing a guy like that. It was way too funny to be as horrible as it sounds. Too funny to even help. I guess the only thing funnier would be if the creek were to rise. It was beginning to rain. Charles was starting to beg.

The rest of us huddled under an old piece of tarp we kept rolled-up and stashed at the fishing hole for just such occasions. Our first impulse was to just leave Charles there and go on back to the clubhouse. If Charles freed himself then we would eventually see him back there. If not, then "we hadn't seen him all day". That sounded good on paper but just as we gathered our gear to leave, Bill stopped in his tracks and said, "Tales from the Crypt."

No explanation was necessary. We all knew *exactly* what he meant. The implication was as obvious as it was ominous. A similar situation had arisen in the latest issue of "Tales from the Crypt". The only difference was, that story had taken place in a real swamp. I think it goes without saying how that one turned out.

Ultimately we cut the line just above the hook and left. We'd read enough Tales From The Crypts to know if Charles couldn't untangle himself from that point then the Crypt Keeper would surely side with us in the matter. Fair enough. So Charles survived that one but...you know how grownups always tell you if you get a hook in you then you'll have to go to the hospital so they can "cut it out"? Well, there you go. It gets worse.

On yet another occasion, we were all up playing in the old Goodwin barn. The Goodwins didn't live there anymore. Hadn't for years. The main house had at one time been nothing short of a mansion. Now it was just an old dilapidated house that nowadays would probably be listed as a "previously enjoyed" home. Now, it was haunted.

The barn, on the other hand, stood several hundred feet behind the main house. With huge openings where once had hung massive barn doors and missing the occasional plank along the outside walls, it was airy and well lit. Totally monster-proof. The Goodwin barn was quite possibly the best place on the planet for playing "Old Mans' Tag". If you're one of those people who don't know how to play Old Mans' Tag then you're an idiot — but I'll explain it anyway.

First off: it must be decided who is "first IT". By convention whoever was the "first one tagged" in the last game — be that five minutes ago, a week ago, a month ago, whatever — is "first IT". If that particular kid isn't present then you start from scratch with "eenie, meenie, minee mo" or "one potato, two potato". If the kid who *should have been IT* shows up later then he is automatically IT when he arrives *and* is "first IT" next game. Anybody else who happens to show up mid-game is just IT.

Whoever is determined to be "first IT" must then remain stationary while counting to one hundred by fives. This gives everyone else twenty seconds to "get away" — officially starting the game.

From this point Old Mans' Tag proceeds like any other kind of tag except, once tagged you must yell, "I'm IT," loud enough for all to hear. Now you're *both* IT. When the next guy gets tagged then you're *all three* IT and so on until everyone is IT. The last one tagged is the winner.

It doesn't take many games to establish a hierarchy (not unlike NASCAR) ranging from the best ("first climber") to the worst ("last climber"). For years I was "third climber" and a constant threat to take the number two position from Eddie Walton. The term "climber" may seem odd to those who have never played Old Mans' Tag in a barn (or on heavy construction equipment) but it is in fact quite proper. We were virtually spiders. I have personally played many a game wherein my feet never so much as touched the ground. We even had a spin-off version called "Old Mans' Poison Tag" — the only difference between that and regular Old Mans' Tag being...the ground is *poison* so if you touch the ground then you're automatically IT. If you're already IT and you touch the ground then you're OUT. This particular version of the game can be very dangerous and definitely *not* for beginners. If you're not an excellent climber then you shouldn't even ask to play.

To fully understand the danger of Old Mans' Poison Tag and the beauty of the Goodwin barn you really need a photograph but I'll do my best to describe it.

Picture a moderate sized, gray (used to be red a thousand years ago) Old MacDonald type barn. Nothing fancy. About fifty feet long and thirty feet wide. In the middle of the longer side you'll find a doorway about ten feet wide and about ten feet high, the doors to which have long since vanished except for part of one laying off to one side, weeds growing around and through it.

As you enter through this doorway you will see an identical opening directly ahead of you on the other side of the barn. This architecture allowed a farmer — presumably Old Man Goodwin — to drive a tractor pulling a hay-wagon into the barn and offload a bunch of hay or feed or oats or whatever farmers offload in barns, before driving straight on through and out the other side without having to back up or turn around.

If you look to your right, at the far end of the barn you'll see a row of stables or small rooms or places where you might put cows. The ceilings of these rooms serve as the floor to the wide-open loft above. If, instead of looking to your right, you look to your left, you'll see the same arrangement at the other end of the barn. The middle area of the barn is a wide-open thirty foot by thirty foot space, empty except for a few piles of old barnwood full of big rusty nails. A very simple layout.

There is no ceiling, just a tin roof, the peak of which is about thirty feet or so above the dirt floor. There are smaller window-looking doorways at each end of the barn, above the lofts, that overlook the barnyard. These undoubtedly were designed to allow access to the loft from the outside or for ventilation or possibly both. I don't really know much about farming but my guess is you probably want to handle stuff on a *first in first out* basis in addition to wanting to keep *whatever* you put up in a loft as dry as possible.

Extending outwards a couple feet from the top of these loft doorways were what I can only describe as *davits*. Davits are those things they hang lifeboats on and these obviously functioned in the same manner; that is, a block and tackle could be rigged that would allow you to hoist heavy objects up to (or down from) the loft, from outside the barn.

The only other thing I probably should point out about the old Goodwin barn is (and this is important)...suspended from the ridge and running the length of the barn, that is to say, from davit to davit, was a very heavy-duty metal track. Hanging from this track — not unlike a monorail car at Disney World — was a forged, solid steel car sporting a three foot piece of rope with a big knot at the bitter end. This too was extremely heavy duty. With an arrangement such as this, one could conceivably lift a heavy object up from the ground and in through the loft doorway at one end of the barn, drag it with a rope the entire length of the track and then lower it back to the ground through the other loft doorway. The whole apparatus was, in fact, structurally sound enough to hold many kids, if you see where I'm going with this.

There were many ways to go from the lofts to the stables below (and vice-versa) without touching the ground. The easiest way was to simply climb down one of the ladders — constructed of one-by-fours attached directly to the front of the lofts — swing through one of several access doorways and hand-walk *monkey bars style* to the far side of the room. From there you had your choice of several holes in the overhead loft floor if you needed to escape. Lots of options. Kids were constantly popping their heads up through these holes to see where everyone else was — kinda like that game where moles pop their heads up out of holes while you try to whack them with a mallet before they can duck back down.

One of the lofts had a long rope suspended from an overhead timber. The proper use of this device was to hold onto it until someone tried to tag you, at which time you would elude your pursuer by simply taking a one or two step running jump and swinging out over the open space *buccaneer style*. Leaping in one direction took you to the opposite end of the loft. This netted a four to five second advantage because whoever was after you had to avoid a number of holes and dry-rotted spots in order to get to the same place. Plus, you still had the rope. It is nearly impossible for one person to tag a skilled climber who possesses the rope.

Leaping in the other direction, on the other hand, allowed you to swing over to the proverbial *broad side of the barn* atop the main doorway — at which point you would "stick to the wall". "Sticking to the wall" was accomplished by supporting your weight with your toes on the two-by-four stringer below while maintaining a firm fingertip grip on the stringer above. While swinging to the side of the barn nets about the same time advantage as the previous maneuver there are several drawbacks.

First and foremost, when you attempt this move you pretty much have to commit to it. Chickening out at the last second means penduluming back to being instantly tagged — not to mention the reputation hit that comes part and parcel with losing one's nerve in front of the guys. On the other hand, it's pretty much a one shot deal and, once committed, is nearly impossible to do without relinquishing control of the rope. Minus the rope you're working without a net.

Once stuck to the wall, however, you can edge your way to nearly any place in the barn — including the other loft — without touching the ground, hence the term "climbers" and the analogy to spiders. This is where it gets interesting. The *poison* version of Old Mans' Tag raises the game to a level of sophistication unequaled by any other kids' game. As more and more kids become IT the game becomes nothing short of three-dimensional Pac Man.

The essence of successful climbing lies rooted in one's knowledge of typical American barn design and the construction practices used to erect these structures. To truly excel at Old Mans' Poison Tag one must possess a keen understanding of barn wall fabrication — the gist of which is as follows:

You begin by digging holes denoting the corners then several structural points along the wall — spaced to support loft timbers, doorway frames, etc. Into these holes massive support poles are planted. Employing mortise and tenon joinery, these poles are connected to each other at their bases by heavy hewn timbers — then capped with more heavy timbers along the top. Two-by-fours known as *stringers* are then run horizontally the entire length of the wall. In the case of the Goodwin barn there were four stringers — the top stringer, the bottom stringer, and two middle stringers (known as the upper middle stringer and the lower middle stringer).

Starting at one end of this skeletal structure, the wall is subsequently sheathed with vertical planks fastened side by side to the stringers until you get to the other end. That's it. If you do this all the way around and slap a roof over it you'll have a typical American barn.

After that, you have forever to add lofts and rooms for cows or horses or pigs or whatever farmers need rooms for. Over the years ladders and hand-holds would be nailed up or notched out or otherwise made to exist at various strategic points throughout the barn — each intended to increase efficiency or generally make it easier for farmers to do what all needs to be done.

The four stringers running the length of each wall inherently defined three routes from the loft at one end of the barn to the loft at the other end — the high, middle and low — of which the middle was the preferred route.

The bottom route was the easiest and least dangerous but of course at some point you had a huge doorway to contend with. This required shinnying up one of the poles, crossing over above the doorway, then shinnying back down the other side.

The high route was obviously the most dangerous of the three and (at least at one end of the barn) was home to a big hornets nest. Scary big. Tangling with a hornets nest whilst clinging to a wall twenty feet or so above the ground is, in my opinion, to be avoided. One time we tried to knock it down with rocks but that didn't work and we ended up running for our lives. After that the hornets seemed to keep a somewhat closer eye on us. Hornets can smell fear you know.

So, there were three basic ways on each side of the Goodwin barn to move from the loft at one end to the

loft at the other end without touching the ground —
each route having its own unique advantages and
disadvantages. Also bear in mind that while "stuck to
the wall" it is virtually impossible to tag someone below
you.

But there was one more way to get from one loft to
the other. This was known as "riding the track" and
was generally accepted to be the method of last resort.
It was easy, at least on paper. All you had to do was
grab hold of the rope attached to the car riding on the
overhead track; take a good running jump from the loft
and (hanging on for dear life) glide over the great
expanse — alighting gracefully on the loft at the
opposite end of the barn. It was at once graceful,
elegant and outrageously cool. It was also potentially
lethal.

Riding the track fundamentally presented three ways
to die. The obvious one was simply to slip off the rope.
Of course, any kid who did that was fairly deserving of
the consequence.

The second way to die was if you went too fast. This
almost happened to me the first time I tried it. What
happens is...you glide past the far loft (this particular
conveyance has no brakes) and out the far window.
Fortunately the car slams into a *stop* at the end of the
track and, *if* you are able to hang on, you'll swing back
in through the window. If you can't hang on then
you're in big trouble. I'll never forget watching the
window frame passing by then, with a *jerk*, finding
myself nearly horizontal on the rope staring down —
not at the ground (that would be bad enough) but
rather at a pile of old wringer washers and other
assorted junk that had accumulated over the years

outside the barn. I still wake up nights looking down at that embodiment of pain and suffering.

The third way to die was in some respects the worst. The worst because you had plenty of time to contemplate your own doom. The third way to die was by going too slow. Enter Charles.

Charles was as poor at climbing as he was at everything else except maybe talking crap. For months he'd talked about how he had *rode the track when nobody was around* but just didn't *"feel like it right now"*. Normally we would goad a big mouth braggart like that into "proving it" but not in Charles' case. Idiot that he was, I think we all instinctively knew that no good could come of it. Somehow we would all end up getting beat for knowing better than to *put him up to it*. You know how that one goes.

Well, apparently our *lack* of interest had the same effect as goading, prompting Charles — against all of our warnings to the contrary — to *prove it* anyway. Before we could stop him he took off across the loft with the rope. My guess is, as the great expanse began looming large in front of him Charles lost his nerve, resulting in what amounted to a fairly lame, half-hearted running jump. We all knew from the git-go he'd never make it. Not enough inertia. The physics just weren't there.

Sure enough the car ground to a sickening halt about halfway down the track leaving Charles to dangle twenty feet or so above the heap of old rusty-nail-laden barnwood planks. I have to admit, at least on some level, it was a relief to know exactly which of the myriad disastrous outcomes would manifest itself. Now we knew. Once again Charles was stuck. Once again we knew we were all going to be in big trouble for being at the Goodwin barn. Just for being with Charles. Our only possible saving grace would be that we'd tried to stop him — precisely *because* we all knew better.

Any one of the rest of us kids, given the same situation, could have scooted our way either to the far end or returned to the start depending on which was closer. Normally, every time you swing, the car will scoot about six inches. As you pendulum back in the opposite direction the car will scoot back the same amount. If, however, you get to swinging *just right* you can actually get the car to scoot about six inches in one direction but only scoot back about five and thusly can work your way in either direction one inch at a time. It's a slow tedious process principled as much in art as in science but it works. It doesn't work if you're an idiot and no amount of explaining it from the ground seemed to help.

Tossing him a rope (even if we'd had one long enough) wouldn't help because there would be no way to catch it — at least not for Charles. At one point we even tried to push his feet with a long stick we'd tied together from several shorter ones but that only resulted in getting Charles spinning to the point he threatened to puke on us — so we stopped. We knew that even with the benefit of sitting on that big knot, Charles couldn't last much longer and as much as we dreaded the idea there was really nothing left to do but seek outside assistance. Bobby, being a naturally more sympathetic guy than the rest of us, was chosen to stay behind to keep Charles company while Bill, Eddie and I went to drum up help.

Help came in the form of Charles' old man. I guess that was good, he was after all an Air Force doctor. He actually thanked us for coming to him first. The fact is, he just happened to be standing in his open garage when we tried to walk by unnoticed. Military doctors (at least in those days) had a reputation for being officers in name and rank *only* and beyond that were pretty much considered butchers amongst the enlisted troops. We were about to find out why as we all headed back up to the Goodwin barn.

As we neared the barn, Bobby and Charles were already coming out. Both were limping, Charles with a big rusty 10d common nail protruding from the side of his head. There was surprisingly little blood, I thought, for as bad as it looked.

All Bobby said was, "I tried to catch him."

Without a word Charles' old man took a calm, experienced, cursory look at Charles' head then promptly marched him back to his garage. There he held Charles' head down on a workbench and pried out the nail with a pair of channel-lock pliers levered over a woodblock. Then he told Charles to "knock off the damn whining," go wash up before his mother got home, and grab the bandages on his way back.

Charles' old man thanked us again for coming to him first and that was it. Done deal. I don't know what all was said but it never went any further than that. We didn't get into any trouble or anything. Charles' old man was a lot cooler than his kid.

That was the last time we ever saw or heard from Charles. Not long afterwards we noticed their house was empty and they were gone. As I mentioned earlier, probably for the best.

The moral of the story is this: anybody who insists on being called Charles (or Theodore or Bartholomew or Timothy, etc.) even when their parents aren't around, is to be avoided. They are walking death magnets.

So, by this point you're probably wondering, "What could any of this possibly have to do with *logistics?*"

The obvious fact is, it has *everything* to do with logistics. It has *everything* to do with logistics *precisely because* it has *nothing* to do with logistics. Charles was gone. That renders the lion's share of a whole chapter on logistics moot. Without Charles there was no reason to worry about bandages, tourniquets, pliers, antibacterial ointments, and unknowns too numerous to even mention in a single book.

After due consideration, it was decided that we already possessed the necessary supplies to make the trek to Paradise Island and beyond — two pocketknives (a hedge against a possible dinosaur encounter), half a canteen of Kool-Aid and one giant econo-pack of Tootsie Rolls. That should do it. The logistics were covered.

12

The Night Before

It was Friday morning when we all gathered at the clubhouse to finalize preparations for our upcoming journey. Several details had yet to be hammered out, the most important of course being — how to not get caught.

After much discussion we decided that our best bet would be to camp out in the field behind Dave's house that night. That way we could avoid the iffy and time consuming prospect of getting everyone together at the same time and same place the following morning. Way too many things could go wrong if we waited until morning to coordinate the outset of our quest.

For instance, you could end up mowing the lawn, or having to stay home to work on some project your mother suddenly deems critical to life on Earth. Just having to be home at noon because Aunt so-and-so is coming to visit, "and you know she hasn't seen you since you were *this high*," could derail even the best strategy.

The simple act of trying to get up and out of the house early could arouse suspicion if not handled tactfully. You have to maintain your cool. You have to act like it's just another ordinary day — but not so ordinary you look like a bored little rich kid who needs a life lesson in working around the house. There's a fine line between the two. At the same time, you cannot allow yourself to *look* like you're trying *not* to look a certain way. You have to have a *normal kid look*. That's not so easy when the big day arrives. You don't want to dash out of the house, letting the screen door slam behind you — unless of course that's what you normally do, then you *have* to do it. That's the kind of edge we're walking here. But...

Tomorrow would be Saturday. That meant most of our folks would likely be *sleeping in*. That's always a good thing for kids. Even though school was out for the summer (and had been for a couple months) parents still tend to think in terms of *school nights* so being a Friday night was bound to work in our favor.

The primary advantage of camping out in the field behind Dave's house was obvious; Dave lived in the last house on a dead-end street. That should significantly diminish the odds of parents stopping *on their way by* to check on us kids. Parents like to do that, you know. On the other hand, making a special trip to the end of the road and parking in front of someone else's house just to check up on a kid who's only been gone a couple hours signals to the other parents in the neighborhood that he's an incorrigible loser — raised by loser parents. Parents *don't* like to do that.

Another plus to spending the night camping behind Dave's house was Dave's old man. On other occasions Dave's old man had actually come out, arranged some big rocks into a circle and started campfires for us saying, "Every boy should know how to do this kinda stuff. Just keep that fire inside the rocks." Then he'd leave us alone for the rest of the night. Dave's old man was really cool.

All things considered, camping out seemed like a solid plan. After all, we hadn't done it in awhile and our folks would probably jump at the chance to get rid of us for the night. Naturally, any time wasted in the morning would serve to limit our maximum travel radius which we reckoned to be only half a day at best. In a situation like this it simply would not do to get home late. Little kids' stories crumble in a hurry when otherwise disparate parents decide to compare notes and that's exactly what happens when enough kids get home late — guaranteed. That's how rookies get caught.

And speaking of getting caught...as we huddled over our official "round table" (actually it was an old telecommunications cable spool) Dave's Aunt Connie, with her gift for prophecy, said, "It's an island."

The rest of us boys, typical of our manner, stared in confusion. We generally did stare in confusion whenever Dave's Aunt Connie first broached a topic but we knew she always thought stuff through before taking center stage and waited for her explanation. I think she kind of enjoyed her ritualistic shtick. We'd humor her. It was usually worth it. Working her little standup routine she continued...

"Well, if it's an island then it's surrounded by water, right?"

She was right.

"So, if it's surrounded by water then we can't very well get to it without getting wet, right?"

Right again. Hmmm, she had a point. A good one. There's no way we can all come home wet and expect to get away with it. There are lots of ways you can talk your way out of coming home muddy, but soaking wet? Swim to an island and back wet? No way.

"Sooo..." digging into her canvas bag (Dave's Aunt Connie always had a bag — not a purse — a bag) she brought out a fistful of plastic dry-cleaning bags she'd been collecting over the years — a hedge against this very circumstance. Now, that may not seem a big deal nowadays but you have to keep in mind that back then there weren't any plastic garbage bags. They simply didn't exist. In fact, I distinctly remember my old man sitting at the kitchen table one morning, reading a newspaper article and saying, "You've got to be kidding me. Nobody *in their right mind* is gonna go out and buy plastic bags just to put their garbage in and then just throw them out. No way."

Now that I think of it, this was the same guy who said nobody *in their right mind* was ever gonna buy a cigarette lighter then, when it runs out of juice, just throw it away, either. Of course it turns out in both cases he was right. Nobody *in their right mind* ever did.

Peeling one of the bags from the wad, Dave's Aunt Connie spread it out on the table in front of us explaining...

"See? I ironed the top shut where the hanger poked through so they can't leak. When we get there we can just put all our clothes and stuff in the bags, tie them shut and swim over to the island. They should all be dry."

It did occur to me that she'd said *should* be dry instead of *would* be dry — but only years later.

To tell you the truth, we boys had sort of figured Dave's Aunt Connie wouldn't even go along at all — her usually being so rational — but in fact, she was way ahead of us. She was full of contradictions like that. Once again Dave's Aunt Connie had proven her worth to the fraternity of guys who were the Eggless Club. She may well have saved us all a good beating.

Then pretty much as an afterthought, Dave's Aunt Connie reached back into her bag of tricks and pulled out a box of kitchen matches, "I thought we might need these too," tossing them onto the table. Bobby, Don, Dave, Bill and I followed suit — each reaching into our pockets and pulling out a pack or two of matches. We were on top of that one. Not so much for survival reasons mind you but because fires were cool. Fires were cool unless, of course, you were Charles.

The mere *sound* of Dave's Aunt Connie's box of kitchen matches hitting the table made all of us guys smile and shake our heads. We were grinning because of Charles. Charles was gone, yet he wasn't. He was still around in spirit. In the spirit of stupid stuff.

One night we were, oddly enough, camping out in the field behind Dave's house. In the wee hours of the morning we decided to go wandering around the neighborhood just because neighborhoods look cool and really different when you're wandering around in the wee hours of the morning. At the first appearance of car headlights we'd melt into the shadows of the ditches on either side of the road. Unseeable. Unknowable. Cool stuff like that. Once the car passed, we'd wait a few seconds...then the mission would resume.

The problem was Charles. He'd brought along a huge box of kitchen matches that he'd crammed into his pocket. Why he'd brought them is anybody's guess but he had them. The trouble was, with each step Charles' pocket would scream, "shik shik, shik shik...." At three o'clock in the morning in our quiet neighborhood he might as well have been a Buick with no muffler. The sound seemed to resonate for miles. After not too long, it occurred to all of us at once that the noise was — *this* idiot. We stopped in the middle of the street. It instantly got quiet.

"Man, you gotta *do* something with those matches."

"Yeah man, you gotta *do* something with those matches — you're gonna wake up the whole neighborhood."

So, Charles took the matches out of the box and stuck everything back into his pocket. I have to admit it was somewhat quieter but the loose matchsticks were still slapping up against the empty box and after a few steps we all agreed it was still too loud.

"Look, Charles, why don't you put the matches in one pocket and put the box in your other pocket? That way they won't rattle around."

That seemed like a good idea and it would be a good idea — for anyone but Charles.

Charles' misfortune began when he pulled the empty box from his pocket. Apparently the striker part of the box rubbed up against one of the matches. It turns out, when you have a whole pocketful of matches you really only have to get one of them started to cause a scene.

The next thing you know, in a demonstration of critical mass worthy of Enrico Fermi, Charles' leg lit up like a road flare. So now Charles was hopping around hollering and lighting up the night sky with his stupid leg. Dogs are barking. Lights are turning on up and down the street. None of this is conducive to stealth operation so — finding it nearly impossible to "shhhhshh" a guy with his leg on fire — we ran. Trying to run and laugh at the same time with the shrieking fires of Hell hot on your tail — doing its level best to keep up — is an experience one does not soon forget.

Again, the mere sound of the box of kitchen matches landing on the table was enough to bring it all back and we stood in our clubhouse laughing like maniacs. The *hang on to something or you'll fall down* kind of laughing. About the time we'd stop...we'd all start up again...and so it went.

We eventually settled down and got back to the pressing business at hand — getting our parents' blessing for the campout. For that we had to pair off into various kid combinations depending upon which of us was currently on the best terms with a particular kid's parents. That meant Bill and I went with Bobby; Dave and Bobby went with me; and so on. Don, who was a year older than the rest of us, went with everyone. Of our lot he was the kind of kid who tended to act the most responsibly, at least in our parents' eyes.

Naturally the story was that *everyone else's parents had already agreed to the idea* thus allowing us to focus inordinate kid pressure on the "last" parent — each parent, of course, being the "last" parent. Standard tactic.

Dave was a shoo-in because the whole thing would be happening practically in his back yard. Only a horrible parent would leave him to pine in his window all night watching all the other kids having a good time barely two hundred feet from his own house. Dave's Aunt Connie of course, wouldn't be camping with us because she never did but she'd be there to hang out for awhile around the campfire. Come morning she would be up early and raring to go. In the meantime, we all knew Dave's Aunt Connie could be counted on to act as a dependable lookout — just another task she considered an elemental component of paying her dues to be part of an otherwise exclusively boys organization. A mission she took very seriously.

By five o'clock that afternoon we'd made the rounds and (thanks to our strategy of overwhelming kid pressure) everyone had been granted permission to camp out — with a couple caveats. Eddie was still visiting his grandparents. We knew that already but we stopped to ask anyway because there was the outside chance he could get back any minute. Plus, if other parents were to inquire of Eddie's old lady then she would at least be privy to the *big campout*. If she were to come off as being surprised by the whole idea it could easily cast a shadow of suspicion upon all of us. It also made her feel good to know her kid was invited and she'd probably miss her sweet little Eddie a little more — thus life in general might be incrementally better for Eddie when he did return.

Bill, on the other hand, was given permission to camp out but was reminded of his pending dentist's appointment in the morning and also that a Saturday opening at the dentist (even in those days) was probably a once in a lifetime stroke of good fortune. To Bill it had little to do with good fortune. It turned out he'd known about the appointment for weeks but had been living in a state of denial.

The facts on the ground were: Bill would be there in the morning to stoke the fire suggesting an occupied campsite while the rest of us could conceivably get an even earlier start. Moreover, he'd be available to put out the word in the morning that we'd "left at daybreak to play with the Catholics" — the final agreed upon plan already involved heading out in their general direction anyway. Short of having a body on their

116

hands, none of our parents ever seemed eager to initiate social contact with the Catholics' parents. I think folks tend to not trust other folks who they perceive as not trusting them. That plus after all, the Catholics were rarely responsible for making *us* late or getting *us* into trouble — it was almost always the other way around.

The remaining daylight hours were dedicated to setting up tents, gathering firewood, pounding the dust out of sleeping bags, filling lanterns with oil and other such truck.

Sure enough, promptly at dusk Dave's old man came out and lit the campfire for us. There's no reason in the world why we couldn't have done it ourselves but he really enjoyed showing us how to do it for the umpteenth time — first placing some wadded up newspaper in a heap then covering that with a stack of small twigs followed by larger kindling. Having some big chunks of dried limbs and scrap two-by-fours at the ready is important but you don't put those on until you get a good little flame going, otherwise it'll just go out. He'd always explain how heat rises, so getting the flame going underneath the big pieces of wood was the key to the perfect campfire.

Of course, we already knew all of this but it was still fun to watch the master at work and listen to the detailed explanation — not only what to do and how to do it but what each step in the procedure was intended to accomplish. I think by growing up in New York City, Dave's old man had never really gotten the chance to do that kind of stuff until he got old so tossing him a bone seemed the least we could do considering how he was really cool and all. Once again Dave's old man told us to "Keep that fire inside the rocks" then disappeared for the night. We were alone. No folks. No adult supervision.

We'd hung lanterns in each of the three pup tents and lit them. We weren't actually in the tents but they looked really cool at night when lit from inside. They looked warm and cozy and even though it was near the end of summer there was that *outside in the middle of the night* chill in the air. Poking the fire with long skinny pokin' sticks until glowing embers had caught on their ends, we used them to make figure eights and write our names in the night sky. Persistence of vision is curious stuff.

Dave went into his old man's garage and came back with a bucketful of sawdust. The deal with sawdust is: you take a handful (no more than that) then, standing up straight, tomahawk spike it into the campfire and command, "Wizard!" The sawdust goes up in a blinding flash accompanied by an impressive "poof". Really cool.

Bringing out marshmallows, Hershey bars and Graham crackers — all the fixin's for smores — Dave's Aunt Connie once again reminded us how blessed we were to have her in our club. Things mellowed after that as we all sat around the campfire. The stories began to flow.

Bill told one of a zillion variations on that one about a couple of teenagers on lover's lane who heard strange noises around their car then [your story here] only to get home later and find a prosthetic hook covered in blood hanging from their car door handle.

Don told about the nursing students who decided to scare their new roommate. They got an arm from wherever they get arms from and tied it to the on/off string of their dorm room light. Apparently they all fell asleep while waiting in the dark for their roommate to return and reach for the light cord. When they awoke the next morning the arm was gone — along with their roommate. They subsequently found her in the utility closet at the end of the hallway, gnawing on the arm — her hair turned completely white.

Naturally, I retold the story of Johnny Eyeball and after that our conversation turned to Paradise Island, and beyond.

We'd found some fairly straight solid sticks while looking for firewood so we took turns using the pocket knives to fashion the sticks into sharp spears — holding the tips over the campfire to harden them. Bill said it was an old Indian trick — I guess he ought to know —and obviously you can't expect to fight off a dinosaur using a stick with a soft point.

Sitting around the campfire perfecting our weapons, we talked about what we might find and even if we'd find anything at all. Could it all be just myth? Bobby and I had already gotten burned on the pre-Civil War treasure hadn't we? Still, what were the odds of Wino, Stokes and Billy Marsh all talking about the same place if it didn't exist — a conspiracy that elaborate seemed unlikely didn't it? How much is a diamond or a ruby or an emerald as big as your fist — maybe even bigger — worth anyway? Is it worth a bicycle? Maybe a house or a football?

Finally deciding those questions and more would be answered tomorrow and that *the sooner we get to sleep, the sooner tomorrow will get here*, Dave's Aunt Connie went home and we guys crawled into our tents. The best thing to do would be to put out the lanterns and try to get some sleep. It wouldn't be easy. It wasn't easy.

13

The Morning Of...

I awoke shivering. It wasn't cold but hard as we tried we'd hardly gotten any sleep at all that night and it showed in our demeanor. Daybreak found us huddled around the circle of rocks, draped in wrinkled sleeping bags and stoking the dying remnants of the campfire. The fire was happy to start up again, not even requiring a match. The ground around the perimeter of the rocks was warm and toasty and it felt good but, unlike the campfire, we weren't coming back to life quite so readily. Today was the day. If ever we needed clear heads it would be today. Dave's Aunt Connie came to our aid — showing up with a thermos of hot cocoa and a stack of cups.

Owing no doubt to her abnormal DNA, she'd gotten plenty of rest and had been up for a while toiling over the brew. Remember, this was years before the advent of Swiss Miss pre-sweetened instant hot chocolate and making the *real thing* on a stove was not something we boys would have even attempted. It wouldn't even occur to us to try. For that matter, even if we'd known how to do it we probably wouldn't have done it anyway. In many ways Dave's Aunt Connie was like having an extra Mom around — minus the downside. We all knew one day she'd sour but in the

meantime it really was kinda nice having her around —
most times anyway — and that morning was one of
those times.

The cocoa worked its magic as the sun crept above
the tops of the cornfield to our East. The sun comes
up in the East. Applying the "Never Eat Slimy Worms"
bit, without actually standing up to do it, I remember
feeling for probably the first time in my life, "I actually
know where I am on the planet." It really did make
sense. I think they should consider dedicating some
kindergarten time to the Cartesian model of coordinate
systems. Why not? Maybe I'll suggest that next time if,
heaven forbid, I'm ever coerced into attending another
PTA meeting. If nothing else, it should quash their
attempts to solicit my participation in their stupid little
brainstorming pow-wows. It's bad enough making little
kids fidget and stew in a classroom for six hours a day
— nearly ten months of the year — without spending
Wednesday nights conspiring to make it even more
repugnant than it already is. Yeah, I'm a *hit* with those
folks.

At any rate, fortified with a more concrete sense of
my relationship to the rest of the universe, I felt my
initial enthusiasm returning. I don't know if the other
guys too had been thinking about the Slimy Worm
concept (it might have been just the caffeine) but we all
found a sudden burst of energy and began gathering
our stuff for the trek. We made our tents, sleeping bags
and so forth look like *we'd be back in a minute* then the
last thing we did was shove each other around a little
bit to make sure nobody's gear rattled. It's not good to
rattle. Ask Charles.

Bill in the meantime hadn't said a word all morning.
He knew perfectly well what all he had to do in our

stead before going off to die a horrible, painful death at the dentist's office so...no sense pressing him on it. No sense rubbing it in. No sense reminding him that at least he'd get to die in a really cool chair. Given the circumstances, a simple, "Well, it's been nice knowing you," seemed enough and, spears in hand, we headed out for the great unknown.

Keeping a keen eye on the relationship between Bill's house and the water tower painted with our community's name "Berwick" (followed by the word "Stokes" scrawled in black paint underneath), we mentally maintained a straight line tangent to both — that was north. Salty sea captains call this *sighting a range*. We called it *keeping a line that points north*.

Normally when heading in the direction of the Old Johnson farm we would circumnavigate the Catholics' turf. They being the last to move into the area, we naturally held controlling share of all the local fields but we felt they had to have *something* to call their own. It was only fair. Without their own little piece of land to defend they'd have grown up even weirder than they already were. Plus, with them living right alongside that particular field, it would have been too resource intensive for us to maintain control. It just wasn't worth the hassle.

The problem was, going *around* meant either going *way around* or cutting through a soybean field. Soybeans are horrible things. For one thing, they taste like crap. Corn you could just stop in the middle of a field and eat. Sweet corn was the best but field corn wasn't bad either. You just pick it, husk it and eat it. You could make corncob pipes and smoke the corn silk too. Of course, it tasted horrible and is (we found out years later) a great way to contract trichinosis but smoking it looked cool and was fun to do.

Turnips were OK too — especially the bigger ones. Little ones are too spicy — like purple radishes. Even squash were good enough once cut up, put on sticks and held over a campfire for awhile. A little butter helps.

Soybeans are good for nothing. Sure, hogs might like them but when's the last time you said something "must be good 'cause hogs sure like 'em."? Exactly. Of course, over the last few decades there's been a mad dash to enhance the reputation of soybeans (and soy products in general) with the development of soy burgers, soy "milk", and so on. The whole thing is an abominable hoax. Anyone who says you can't tell the difference between soy burgers and *real* hamburgers should be held underwater until they've completely stopped twitching.

But that's not even the worst part about soybeans. The worst part about soybeans is how they grow. They grow on what can only be described as baling wire. If you've ever heard someone say things went "haywire", that's the stuff they're talking about. Trudging through a field of soybeans is like wading through a sea of tumble weeds. So cutting through the Catholics' turf would not only save us a lot of time and energy but innumerable scrapes and scratches as well. We knew also that, with the exception of the two youngest Cassidi brothers, the Catholics had not yet returned from their Retreat so cutting through their field should be no problem.

Of course it's always best to cut through unnoticed — just on principle — but that would be impossible. From where we were, we could already see John (who they called Jack) Cassidi in his backyard making something out of dirt. Instinctively sensing our approach Jack Cassidi looked up and spotted us. I guess we looked harmless enough — even toting spears with sharpened, campfire-hardened (Indian-style) points — because he actually smiled and came out to greet us.

"Where ya goin'?"

"Nowhere."

"Can I go?"

The question caught us flatfooted. We'd expected just about anything but that. Jack Cassidi go with? We all just kinda looked at each other but before we could say anything Jack Cassidi continued, "Jim ended up going on Retreat. I'm the only one here."

Jack Cassidi was desperate. We all knew he really wasn't such a bad guy and we were short two kids, Eddie and Bill, and we did have the extra spear Bill had made while still in his zombie-like state of denial, so Jack Cassidi could carry that. Plus, he'd already spent two days by himself and had been reduced to playing in dirt — not that there's anything wrong with playing in dirt mind you but this...this was borderline pathetic. We couldn't help but feel sorry for the guy. We didn't really want the responsibility of another little kid but didn't feel we could just walk away from it, so we said, "Sure, but we're gonna be gone all day and you can't know where we're going until we get there. OK?"

"OK sure. Do you want me to get my shovel?"

"Yeah, it'd be a good idea to have a shovel but *you* gotta carry it."

"OK, You guys wait here I'll be right back."

Jack Cassidi ran up to the house to get his shovel. The rest of us left — waiting around would be setting an undesirable precedent — but we deliberately took our time, giving him a sporting chance to catch up easily, and we left Bill's spear sticking in the ground so Jack Cassidi wouldn't think he'd misunderstood the upshot of our discussion. It seemed only fair to let him tag along after cutting through his turf and all; it seemed the Christian thing to do. Plus, if sacrificing a kid to an irate dinosaur should become necessary then well, let's just say that weighed heavily in our decision to allow John (who they called Jack) Cassidi to join our entourage.

Within minutes Jack Cassidi had caught up with us and fallen in — equipped with a pocketknife, his old man's genuine U.S. Army entrenching tool and Bill's spear. Now there were six of us. Don, Dave, Bobby, Dave's Aunt Connie, the youngest Cassidi brother (Jack) and me.

After Jack Cassidi joined us we picked up the pace a little bit — not that we needed to but because, as the past trailed off behind us and our future rose up in front, an air of anticipation began to permeate the atmosphere. We felt good. Excited. Poor Jack Cassidi was visibly straining to not ask where we were going and strangely it was getting more and more difficult not to tell him. The next waypoint would be halfway between the bottom of Schwartz Hill and the Old Johnson farm.

Periodically looking back to check the relationship of Bill's house to the water tower — the house became harder and harder to distinguish from the surrounding landscape. The tall oak tree in Eddie's yard next door to Bill's clearly stood out from the other trees and soon replaced Bill's house as our navigational aid. Of course, the water tower itself was clearly visible for miles — even at night.

Like a cherry on top, the water tower boasted a bright red flashing light used to warn low-flying aircraft of its presence in the dark. There was a small private airfield only a few miles away that was home to a handful of Piper Cubs, one twin-engine Cessna and a few old crop dusting biplanes, none of which, at least to my recollection, ever flew at night. On the other hand, Charles had told us once that one of his old man's Air Force pilot buddies told him they used to take a bearing off that water tower all the time when approaching Lockborne Air Force Base from the north. At any rate, as long as you kept moving toward the Berwick water tower — day or night — you could get home. Knowing that, the world wasn't nearly as big and scary as it could have been, even at night. One night in particular it came in handy. Real handy.

We were heading to a point halfway between the bottom of Schwartz Hill and the Old Johnson farm. That is to say, we weren't actually going as far as the Old Johnson farm — that was good. It was good because the Old Johnson farmhouse on the Old Johnson farm was (like the Goodwin house) haunted. We knew this to be fact because we had witnessed it ourselves and upon seeing the old place through the trees ahead it all came back to us.

We'd all heard the story. It went like this...

The Johnsons had lived there for generations. The last bunch of Johnson kids was grown and gone and now just the old man and his wife lived there. For years the wife had hounded the old man to build her a sewing room in the basement and now that all the kids were grown and gone she saw no reason why he shouldn't drop everything and do it. I guess she just never let up.

One day she said she would just do it herself, went out and bought whatever fixin's she deemed necessary to build whatever it was she had in mind, and proceeded to just do it herself. This made Old Man Johnson really mad. Where he came from, girls just didn't *do* stuff like that.

She would go out to the garage and carry down a single two-by-four or a single box of nails. Up and down the steps. Over and over again. He was dying to see what she was doing but couldn't bring himself to go look and all the while she spoke not a word. Night after night he got more and more aggravated. The *wham* of each hammer blow piercing his brain. Nail after nail. Two-by-four after two-by-four. Night after night. Up and down the steps. Over and over. She'd pass by him oblivious to his presence and it was gnawing at him — big time.

Then she started making trips up and down the steps with quarts of paint — not gallons — quarts. She was building a sewing room *at* him. Painting a sewing room *at* him. Up and down the steps. Over and over. Quart after quart. Finally...he snapped.

They say it was exactly midnight when Old Man Johnson went out to the barn and, grabbing his surest hog-butcherin' knife, went downstairs to find his wife in the far corner of the basement — painting the wall. Apparently her screams could be heard three and four farms over as he hacked Old Lady Johnson to death in the basement of the Old Johnson farmhouse on the Old Johnson farm. Then he went back out to the barn where they found him hanging the next day.

Now (or so the story goes) if you're in the basement precisely at midnight painting the wall, the ghost of Old Lady Johnson will appear, dripping blood and brandishing the very knife used to kill her that fateful night — seeking revenge on anyone who might be taking over her job of finishing her sewing room.

So, that's the story. We'd all heard it many times from several different sources. One day, after arguing over its validity, we decided to put it to the test. Eddie got a can of paint from his old man's shop (his old man was a painter by trade) along with a couple paintbrushes. That afternoon we, those of us who could anyway, convinced our folks to let us stay overnight at the other's house and (armed with brushes, a can of paint, flashlights and a candle) we went to the Old Johnson farm — intending to be there in the basement painting the wall at precisely midnight.

I have to admit the place seemed pretty normal — in the daytime. It was dangerous of course. The house had long been condemned by the county folks and for good reason. There were rotted spots in the floor, where you could easily fall right through if you didn't step where the joists would support you, and the steps going down to the basement groaned under our slight weight but all and all it was kind of a cool place to check out. Sure enough, the walls of the basement had been painted up to a point, then the paint abruptly ended. That was creepy. Still, it wasn't bad — in the daytime.

Come nightfall, we lit the candle and all sat in a circle on the basement floor telling ghost stories (probably not the best idea we'd ever had) and waiting for midnight. Bobby had a pocket watch — the accuracy of which we'd checked before leaving home

— and was calling out time hacks every few minutes. Three, maybe four hours is an awfully long time to just sit and wait if you're a kid but eventually midnight drew near. We were still laughing and joking but every once in awhile the old house would creak for no apparent reason and we'd stop, listen for a minute...or two...then go back to goofing around.

At around eleven forty-five we opened the can of paint and stirred it with a stick. It was red. We asked Eddie, with all the different colors he had choose from why he had picked red.

"I could swear it was green." That was a little creepy too, but OK.

The wind had picked up somewhat and the house was creaking and groaning a little more than it had been earlier but no big deal. Previously we had flipped coins, odd man out, and Bobby and Dave had won the honor of being the ones actually painting the wall when the time came — at midnight.

At eleven fifty-nine Dave handed his brush to Don and said, "Here, you can do it, I'm kinda tired."

Don didn't want it and offered it to me. I said, "No, Dave won fair and square, he can have it." Turning to offer it instead to Eddie, Don evidently whisked it a little too close to the candle — blowing it out. Apparently that candle was keeping the place warm because as everybody fumbled in the dark for their flashlights the room suddenly felt really, really cold. At one point during all the commotion someone (or some *thing*) latched onto my arm, either trying to find a flashlight or in search of its next meal, I couldn't be sure which, so that didn't help matters.

The first flashlight to light was high-tailing it up the steps and a full-blown panic ensued. Scratching and clawing, we clambered over one another in a mad scramble to get out. One of the steps broke completely in half under Don's weight but it barely slowed him down at all. Within seconds we were all out of that house — scattering in all directions. I guess we were all out; I didn't look back to see. I didn't want to see. Nobody did, as we ran for our very lives.

I ran a long way before finally stopping to get my bearings. It was dark and spooky. Off in the distance, in different directions, I would occasionally spot the flicker of what appeared to be a flashlight but I didn't even attempt to check it out. I just kept going. We all did — moving steadily toward the red blinking light atop the Berwick water tower that also said "Stokes" on it. If you just keep moving toward the blinking red light, you'll make it home. Just keep moving toward the light.

It was a lot cooler outside than when we'd first gotten to the Old Johnson farm — dew had settled on the weeds. It was cold and wet and dark. Spiders come out when it's dark you know.

Within the hour I'd made it to our clubhouse — Don and Dave were already there. Though we hadn't really thought far enough ahead to have a *plan B,* the Eggless clubhouse seemed like the logical place to go. In fact, it was the only place to go. We couldn't very well go home could we? By the time Eddie arrived a few minutes later, our biggest concern was trying not to laugh too loudly — the last thing we wanted was to all get caught at our clubhouse and have it be put off limits.

It was a good hour before Bobby showed up. His flashlight was still back at the Old Johnson farm but somehow he'd made his way back in total darkness.

Good. That was everyone who'd gone. All present and accounted for. Now we could relax. Dragging out a couple blankets and a huge quilt we kept stashed at the clubhouse, we curled up on the floor for the night.

At sunrise we all went to our respective homes, said good morning to everyone then went to bed. The folks actually thought it was *so cute* that we were all *bushed from our slumber party*. It had indeed been a long, memorable night but at least we'd found out what we were trying to find out. Yes, the Old Johnson farmhouse was haunted. No doubt about it. Just like the Goodwin house — there's a reason nobody lives in those places.

Standing at a point halfway between the bottom of Schwartz Hill and the Old Johnson farm — each of us privately reliving his own version of the events of that night — is as close as we would ever get to the Old Johnson farmhouse again.

Our faraway looks didn't escape the notice of Jack Cassidi, prompting him to ask, "What are you guys looking at?"

Except for Bill and Dave's Aunt Connie, nobody who wasn't actually there knew the story. Oh, they all knew the place was haunted alright but nobody outside of the Eggless Club knew of our investigative attempt to unearth the truth, which we did. Jack Cassidi didn't know and we weren't about to tell him. The last thing we wanted was to have Jack Cassidi standing there wondering what he was doing in the middle of nowhere surrounded by a bunch of yellow-bellies. After all, it hadn't exactly been our finest hour, had it? So, we changed the unspoken subject.

"You want to know where we're going?"

"Yeah."

After a quick *cross my heart — hope to die* pact, we all sat in a circle and told Jack Cassidi the whole story. We told him about Wino. We told him about Stokes (yeah, that's the same guy who's on the water tower) and Billy Marsh. We told him about Bill's old man being almost part Indian and north. Dave's Aunt Connie stood up and did her Never Eat Slimy Worms routine. The whole nine yards.

Needless to say, Jack Cassidi was extremely impressed — not just by what we knew but probably more so by *how* we figured out what it was we did know. He'd learned more about logic and reasoning from us in fifteen minutes than he had in his whole life from all of his older brothers put together — coming away (I think, anyway) with a new found appreciation for the sleeping juggernaut known as the Eggless Club.

Just walking through the entire soup-to-nuts account of the events leading up to that very time and place, coupled with Jack Cassidi's immediate and wholehearted enthusiasm, served to rekindle our own passion for the mission.

Our thoughts and ambitions turned to points — due west.

14

Due West

Clouds don't make good landmarks. From our location halfway between the bottom of Schwartz Hill and the Old Johnson farm, we had taken a bearing off a fluffy white formation of cumulus clouds that was (at least at the time) due west of us and we headed in that direction. When we emerged from a stand of trees the clouds had moved — at least we thought they had — it was really hard to say for sure because their appearance had changed dramatically.

Bobby and I thought they were the clouds off to the right. Don and Dave thought they were the ones off to the left. Jack Cassidi didn't have an opinion either way. Dave's Aunt Connie didn't care about clouds at all. She'd taken her bearing off of a high voltage electrical tower standing atop a hill in the far distance — a hill notable for its long history of standing still.

Where I grew up there was always a hill in the far distance. Apparently, a few years back a glacier had moved through our neighborhood — shearing off the tops of the mountains and smoothing them into the rolling hills with which we were all accustomed. A few miles south of us the glacier decided Ohio was too hot and receded back up north. Where it changed its mind, the whole Earth abruptly rises a hundred feet or more, marking the beginning of the Allegheny plateau.

We kids had all been there, either on school field trips or, in my case, at family reunions. We had a lot of hillbillies on Mom's side of the family. They mostly came from the Allegheny Plateau. Genuine hillbillies from genuine hills.

We used to love visiting — especially our cousins Johnny and Jaggie. They had a barn with real live horses and everything. We weren't allowed to ride them or anything but they had a really neat leather saddle sitting on a stand over in the corner and we could ride that. That was almost as cool but not as dangerous.

Their loft had one of those big loft windows like at the Goodwin barn. We'd all lay side by side by side in the hay looking out that window for hours. Not only did it afford a terrific view of the hills but from up there we could watch Johnny and Jaggie's Aunt Becky, out on the front porch of the house, nursing our newest cousin Mike. She was really really pretty and we just loved watching that little baby fatten up.

Whenever we went to visit Johnny and Jaggie they'd take my brother and me to check out really cool stuff. Stuff like meandering creeks and hidden underground caves. Our cousins were allowed to play in the river any time they wanted — without having to ask or anything — and if they got all wet and muddy, no big deal. Hillbillies are great. They don't go by clouds or anything, they just *know* where they're at, even if you blindfold them and spin them around. Jaggie proved it to us one time; you couldn't fool him.

Hillbillies know which plants to stay away from (some of them can really make you itch) and which plants you can eat. They can even tell which kinds of animals live in different holes just by looking at their tracks. I wanted to be a hillbilly too. I still do. I think Johnny and Jaggie were part Indian.

From our second-story classroom at school we could see the plateau rise up to form the horizon and I spent many hours daydreaming about that evidence of geological activity — more than I was allowed. On more than one occasion, Mrs. Hanstein had reprimanded me for not paying close enough attention in her class, pulling down the blinds at that end of the room — seemingly unapologetic about trying to bore me to death. She deserved her nickname — Mrs. *FrankHanstien*. She's the one I hold most responsible for my first beating in a principal's office.

One day Jerry Barnes and I were talking in class — nothing unusual about that. Apparently Mrs. Hanstein was having a bad day. I guess she'd *had it about up to here* with us and sent us out to stand in the hall — me at this end (no doubt so she could keep an *eye* on me) and Jerry Barnes clear down at the other end.

Standing in the hall is incredibly boring. Especially when you're a kid. Especially when you're *me*. Being an elementary school and all, there was absolutely nothing in the hall. No wall lockers. No windows. Nothing but a couple closed doorways leading to other classrooms. The only sign of life at all was a sixth-grade teacher who came up the steps and passed by me on the way to her classroom — glaring at me as if she knew the *whole* story behind our punishment — just *looking* for any excuse to add to it. I didn't give her one. Still, it was the most eventful thing to happen in a long time.

After that we stood there in silence. Silence followed by more silence. It was horrible. I could feel the life ebbing from my body. That's when Jerry Barnes reached into his pocket and pulled out a marble — a brown and yellow, half-pint aggie. Once again life was good.

He rolled the marble in my direction. It was great. Even though he rolled it slowly, it rolled and rolled and rolled. It seemed (with the exception of an occasional hop over an uneven tile) to glide frictionless on the highly polished tile floor — a classic demonstration of the laws governing the conservation of kinetic energy. With only a couple doorways to contend with, you couldn't miss either. That marble would have rolled ten times the length of that hallway if I hadn't been there to stop it. Fascinating. Rolling so slowly, it seemed to take forever getting to my end of the hallway. When it arrived I snatched it up, admired the swirled milky pattern for a second...then rolled it back.

Suddenly being in the hallway wasn't so bad — much better than being in class. Think about it, how often do you have an entire empty hallway all to yourself just to roll a marble in? I could have spent a lifetime rolling that marble back and forth, stopping only for an occasional meal. In a perfect universe that's how it would be...but that's not what happened. What happened was something *less* than perfect.

I had rolled the marble back to Jerry Barnes for the umpteenth time and was waiting for him to roll it back to me when the door opened and Mrs. Hanstein came out into the hall. I'm pretty sure the guilt was gnawing at her for mercilessly making us stand in the hallway watching our lives waste away — young and uneducated. She was busy quizzing me on whether or not I had *learned my lesson* (you know the routine) when...I heard it. As best I can tell, my good buddy Jerry Barnes had *just* let go of the marble when she came out. I could hear it. I could hear the damn thing rolling down the hallway. Faintly at first, then louder. Not loud, mind you, but loud...er. Close...er. The Doppler Effect was taking a toll on my nerves.

Mrs. Hanstein didn't seem to notice. Was it possible? Was this a ray of hope? She was talking; that ought to drown out the noise of a single glass marble rolling frictionless on a hard tile surface, right? Sure, my senses were already attuned to the sound but this old battleaxe — she was half deaf anyway, right? Could that marble just glide on by, totally unnoticed, only to bounce down the steps and into oblivion? No.

What happened next haunts me to this day. At the absolute last second, I looked down to see her pointy, bone-thin, green high-heeled shoe pivot on its spike and descend on the brown and yellow half-pint aggie with a "click" — stopping it in its tracks. A perfect shot. Perfectly timed.

I must have been pale and gaunt when I looked back up at Mrs. Hanstein. She was smiling down at me. No, not a happy smile. This was an evil, blood curdling, spine chilling smile. This was bad. She was a monster.

Lifting a long bony finger, she motioned to Jerry Barnes to "come here". Then looking back to me she said simply, "Come with me."

We went to the main office where Jerry and I were instructed to wait outside; she went in. Standing in the hallway while others determined our fate, I called Jerry Barnes every nasty thing I could think of. It was, after all, entirely his fault. What kind of idiot brings a marble to school anyway?

I'd run out of curse words (an inadequacy I've since corrected) when Jerry was called into the office for one swat. I could hear it. It sounded — not good. And so I waited. Like one of Sinbad's crew waiting to see which guy the Cyclops would come to get next, except...I was the only guy left.

A lifetime later Jerry Barnes came back out. He wasn't exactly crying but his face was flushed and you could tell he wanted to. Without a word he walked gingerly back to Mrs. Hanstein's class. Another lifetime later came my turn.

I was led into Mr. Karnute's office and the door closed behind me. He didn't have much to say but he made sure I saw the paddle. It was a thin, flat, highly polished slat of blond oak with the words "Board Of Education" neatly painted on it. Apparently that's a real knee slapper amongst upper echelon educational types.

Mr. Karnute told me to turn around and grab my ankles. Grab my ankles for crying out loud. I hadn't expected that. Then I was informed that Jerry had gotten *one* swat but I was going to get *two*. I was getting *two* swats because *I* "should have known better". I should have known better, yeah, but not *grab your ankles* known better. Sometimes life just ain't fair. I'd wager when I left the office I looked a lot like Jerry Barnes.

That's where my mind was when I bumped into Dave, who had bumped into Don, who had stopped. We were in a clearing. Ahead lay one remaining small patch of cornfield and beyond that stood a wide swath of old-growth trees that we reckoned could only be Alum Creek.

We took a break. No telling what might lie ahead so it would probably be best to rest-up here; check our gear; make sure everything was in working order before committing to crossing that last patch of cornfield. For Jack Cassidi's benefit we went over the basics. From here on out (until further notice) we would maintain rigid silence. No talking unless it's absolutely necessary and even then, just whisper. Watch where you step. No breaking any big twigs. Don't rattle. Stay low. The usual.

Even though we weren't part Indian or anything, we had the *moving silently through the woods* part down pat. Kids nowadays can't even come close. Even my own grandkids. They try to sneak up on me and I catch them every time. I call them the "elephants". They hate that. I, on the other hand, sneak up on them all the time. They hate that too. They evidently think old guys don't know anything about dirt clods either. Hey, some skills you never lose. I can't wait to show them how all that works one of these days — uppity little snots. We pressed forward in stealth mode.

The last patch of cornfield was exactly that — a patch. That is to say, it was nestled inside the crook of a sharp bend in the river. Like I said, Old Man Bolls left no acreage unplanted. Coming to the edge of the cornrows at the very apex of the river bend, we stopped. From there we'd spread out. Don tapped each of us in passing and pointed — one left, one right, one left, and so forth. Thus with sharpened, campfire-hardened (Indian-style) spears at the ready, we moved out. One each. Quick.

There it was. Paradise Island. It did exist and we had found it — there, not more than thirty feet from our side of the creek. We lay on our bellies, perfectly still. Silent. Looking for any signs of life — in particular, dinosaurs.

Just as Dave's Aunt Connie had predicted, it was indeed an island — technically. It was completely surrounded by water anyway. That we could see the river bottom from where we were meant the water separating us from Paradise Island couldn't have been more than a couple feet deep (it was a muddy creek) except for about the last few steps.

Situated as it was — right at the bend in the creek — it was easy to surmise the events that must have occurred to create the island. It works like this:

A certain amount of water has to make its way down a river one way or another. Whenever there's a bend in a river, a sand bar (or silt bar, or mud bar — whatever you want to call it) forms along the inside of the bend. This forces the current to the outside of the bend. Over many years the current erodes the river bottom making it deeper on the outside of the curve than on the inside. The deeper it gets, the more the sand bar grows. The more the sand bar grows, the deeper and narrower the river becomes along the outside of the bend, and so on. So, there's that.

Then one day years ago, a tree fell into the water and floated downstream, snagging on the sand bar — in effect splitting the river in two. Over time, more and more silt and debris accumulated around the snag, creating the land formation we were looking at — Paradise Island. Between the island and us ran the shallow half of the river. Between the far side of the island and the opposite shore the river was deep.

Once the river had split into two smaller rivers then the same forces of nature were again brought to bear — albeit on a smaller scale — between the island and us. Now we were confronted with shallow water to wade through, except for the last ten feet or so. From where we were we could tell that was a deep trench. But luck was on our side.

Some time in the past, a huge cottonwood tree had given up the ghost — probably in a storm — and toppled over, traversing the deep trench — in essence bridging the middle of the island to the mainland.

After a few more minutes of covert surveillance and passing the OK sign from kid to kid, we quietly made our separate ways down the bank — regrouping at the base of the fallen cottonwood bridge.

We had all seen King Kong and were at that moment on the same wavelength — all thinking the same thing. This tree bridge sure looked a lot like the one those guys tried to cross while tracking the giant ape. Talk about putting all your eggs in one basket. We recognized the obvious flaw in their plan and weren't about to repeat their mistake. We would cross one at a time — not all in a bunch.

15

Paradise Island

So, exactly how safe was it to cross over to the island? That's what we needed to find out. If there were any dinosaurs lying in wait, we needed to flush them out. Picking up a rock, Don held it high enough for all to see and gestured for the rest of us to do likewise — which we did. Silently counting to three on his fingers, Don rose up and heaved his rock into the underbrush along the island's shore. We all followed suit then crouched back down to watch what would happen. Several squirrels scurried up trees. A flight of blackbirds took wing, squawking and flapping their way up the river. Something else rustled its way into the interior of the island but, whatever it was, it was small. Then all fell silent again.

We reloaded and on an audible count of three, repeated the tactic — this time hollering and yelling — ready to dash in the event a Tyrannosaurus Rex should rear up against our intrusion. None did — this time nothing stirred.

Being the oldest and biggest of the Eggless members (not to mention the undisputed number-one climber) Don would be the first to cross the King-

Kong-esque bridge. Along with that obligation would come the honor of being the first of our kind to set foot upon Paradise Island.

Silent, surefooted, he scampered over the makeshift bridge — stopping only momentarily at the sound of one last startled blackbird fleeing for its life. Reaching the other side, Don nimbly climbed down through the maze of gnarled limbs that had once been a treetop and touched down onto the island. The Eggless had landed.

Hunkered down, spear in hand, semi-hidden by the largest of the old cottonwood's limbs, Don studied the terrain for what seemed like a long time before, satisfied with the situation, he waved the rest of us over. One by one we traversed the cottonwood bridge and climbed down onto the island — first one to the left, next one to the right and so on — establishing a beachhead.

It was exhilarating. Wild and unspoiled. Paradise Island was the most exotic place I had ever seen. Even Don — the most serious-minded of our lot — grinned from ear to ear when Dave's Aunt Connie withdrew from her bag a red handkerchief-size flag. Embroidered in white was a single word, "Eggless".

Scaling the tallest upright branch that would support his weight then using the two long leather strips sewn to the corners to attach the flag for all to see — Don announced:

"I hereby claim this island in the name of the Eggless Club. From this day forward may no one ever come to this island without knowing *We* were here first."

Of course, we all knew Wino had been there first but that had been civilizations ago. Besides, Don was always saying cool stuff like that. It was indeed a proud moment — the greatest moment in our club's history — and remained so until years later when Don would earn the Congressional Medal of Honor in the jungles of Southeast Asia — oddly enough, for doing roughly the same thing but that time he would be carrying a wounded buddy with him.

For now, the real celebration would have to wait — we still had an island to secure. Regrouping to weigh our options, we decided to split into three scouting parties. Bobby and I would scout to the south. Dave and his Aunt Connie would move north and Don (being the oldest and the best) would take Jack Cassidi (the youngest and weakest) with him straight through the heart of the island and we would all meet up on the other side. We moved out. Two each. Quick.

Making our way through the tangle of limbs and branches that had once been the treetop of the old cottonwood, Bobby and I emerged on the south side where, still operating in stealth mode, we began our recon of the lower perimeter of Paradise Island. It wouldn't be easy. With nearly the entire shoreline piled with drifted snags, you had to be a really good climber to make any headway. I was.

There's a lot more to climbing than simply pulling with your arms and pushing with your feet — if you've ever blazed a trail through a system of mangrove roots then you know what I'm talking about — and this...this was worse. You have to know *where* to pull and *what* to grab and what *not* to grab, requiring a keen sense of physics and a good eye. Step on the wrong branch, tug on the wrong protrusion of dead root, and the whole world will topple over on you — leaving you to be found later, an unidentifiable heap of bleached bones. Tales From the Crypt fodder.

You have to always keep in mind that *Mother Nature piled this stuff here*. We've all seen the Black Hills (or at least pictures of them) and other similar places where rain and wind-driven sand have conspired over millennia to erode the substrate — leaving behind massive boulders precariously perched atop tall spindly columns of compressed stone. It's a lot like that. You don't want to monkey around with those things either.

Of the two of us, I was considered to be the better climber (remember, I was the number three climber) but it was more than just that. Of our entire club membership, even Don agreed, I possessed the most intuitive sense of naturally occurring stuff. *Touch the wrong thing and you'll stampede the whole herd* kinda stuff. So I took point — Bobby fell back as drag-man.

Thus we advanced, hugging the coastline as best we could — at one point being forced inland in order to circumnavigate one such clump of twisted snags that just had that *look* about it. We could see, lodged up inside, a mangled heap of bones belonging to what we agreed could only have been a dinosaur. Judging by the size, a baby one — no bigger than say, a *small* dog or possibly a *big* opossum. Obviously it had failed to heed the warning. Poking out from the remains, the unfortunate beast's skull seemed to say to me, "Go around." I think I may be part Indian.

It's a good thing we did *go around* too because we discovered a bush loaded with raspberries. After removing my matches, candle, and homemade collapsible spyglass from the ammo pouch on my belt and stuffing them into my pockets, I filled the pouch nearly full with berries and we moved out. Two each. Quick.

Continuing our mission took us back to the water's edge whereupon emerging from the foliage we found ourselves in a small clearing at the southernmost tip of the island — a spit now known as Dinosaur Bone Point.

There the two rivers merged back into one and meandered downstream away from Paradise Island. From there Alum Creek would eventually meet up with the Scioto River, flow into the Ohio River, connect to the Mississippi and — if Tom Sawyer is to be believed — meander all the way to New Orleans. Armed only with sharpened, campfire-hardened (Indian-style) spears and an intuitive sense of stuff that might fall on you, we had discovered a portal to the cosmos.

Sure, Magellan, Vasco de Gama and the like had started the ball rolling but it would be we — the Eggless Club — who would pick it up and advance it from there. From our little island we could theoretically go anywhere in the whole world.

Bobby Stafford and I stood for a long time on Dinosaur Bone Point contemplating the gravity of our discovery. Even though the river had always been there, it was somehow different. I realize now, it was that event — that very instant in time — that spawned within me a wanderlust that would drive (if not haunt) me for the next half century — so far. The world was at our fingertips. Conquering it would be a mere formality. Bobby checked his pocket watch — it was time to press on.

As it turned out, Paradise Island wasn't round at all. Rather it was long and skinny — almost banana shaped. Moreover, the west coast of the island was nothing like the other side. There were hardly any snags and the coast was clear.

Following a thin strip of sand north along the water's edge, we kept a sharp lookout for giant reptiles of any sort in the center of the island. It was common knowledge that Jason and his Argonaut crew didn't see their Dragon until they realized they were standing on top of it! One can never be too careful and now was not the time to lose vigilance.

We hadn't seen any dinosaurs (yet) but scanning the underbrush for any broken symmetry we did find something really cool. There, about halfway up a weed stalk, I recognized a small reddish-brown spherical object. Roughly the size of a golf ball and light as a feather, it looked a lot like a hunk of urethane foam. Urethane foam is that stuff you make in science class by pouring two disparate liquids into a container wherein the mixture reacts by foaming up and over the vessel only to immediately harden into something that looks a lot like a root-beer float — but it isn't.

I'd found one of the curious objects two years earlier. I figured it for a cocoon of some sort and in a way I guess it was. Taking it home, I dropped it into a jar in my bedroom window — expecting a butterfly (or possibly a moth) come spring. That's not what I got.

I had completely forgotten about the oddity until one morning a few months later I awoke to find my bedroom covered with tiny, tiny praying mantises — literally thousands of them.

My mother liked fish. They didn't like her. From time to time throughout my youth she would come home with a brand new batch of fish. Goldfish. Guppies. Zebra-looking things. You name it. They'd always seem to last a little while then one day you'd come home and they'd all be eaten by the biggest one. Not long afterwards, that one too would just up and die — probably from eating so much fish. That was the bad news (at least if you're a fish). The good news was...we had an empty aquarium.

Did you know, if you hold a pencil or just about any little stick in front of a praying mantis, it'll study it for a minute then hop on it? Well, they do. Applying the *hop on the pencil* technique, I collected every one of those critters and put them in the aquarium — covering it with a piece of old window screen.

I couldn't wait to tell the gang and by that afternoon every kid in the neighborhood had stopped by to check out my cool collection of tiny beasts. They look even beastier under a magnifying glass. The first look was free but that was just the hook. After that it cost one pop bottle for a baker's five minutes — a fair price in anyone's book. We were cleaning up.

Everyone agreed praying mantises probably ate grass (remember, this was decades before Wikipedia) so that's what I fed them. Every day I would swap out the old grass for some fresh grass and they seemed to be doing fine. They weren't doing fine. It turns out, praying mantises don't eat grass at all. What they eat is...each other. My herd of praying mantises was diminishing exponentially and before I figured out why, there were but a handful left. Those were getting big.

For the next few days I caught flies and introduced them to the herd. Apparently, praying mantises find themselves tastier than flies and the next thing I knew, the biggest one was in fact the only one. After that, he thought flies were just fine — although he soon graduated to bigger and better prey. Crickets and beetles. Grasshoppers. Flies are a gateway bug.

He might have been the last one alright but he was really cool. If you put a lamp behind his aquarium then gave him something to eat it was like watching through an x-ray machine. You could see each bite go all the way down his long skinny neck and disappear into his fat belly. Really cool. Two pop bottles cool.

One day Bobby, Eddie and I were sitting in the living room watching Captain Kangaroo when Mom came bustling out of the hallway. Pointing back toward my bedroom, all she could say was, "Wh, bo, bo. Wh, bo, bo...."

I guess I'd left the roof off of his house because my praying mantis had gotten loose. Of course, all you had to do was stick out your hand and he'd hop right on but (even though she liked him OK) Mom wasn't about to do that.

Naturally we christened him Wibobo. Later, that was shortened to Wibby or (in the third person) simply — The Wib.

Wibby became the Eggless Club mascot. He'd go everywhere with us just to hang out — one of the gang. Later, he got wings and could fly rather than just walk or hop. He didn't fly much — I guess because he was never much good at it — but if he slipped off of something really high, he'd flutter and flap all the way down and hit the ground, just not hard enough to bounce. He just wanted us to *think* he could fly. We never got on him about it though. He still could fly better than any one of us.

Dave's Aunt Connie really liked Wibby a lot and would take him home to spend the night and stuff. One day Dave's Aunt Connie found a book called "Mantid" and we figured out why. Wibby wasn't a *he* — Wibby was a *she*. It turns out (at least with Wibby's particular genus of Mantidae) if their bellies are comprised of six segments — then they're boys. If their bellies have seven segments — they're girls. Apparently the extra segment is for "girlie bits". We all took turns verifying the count and...Wibby was definitely a girl. After that, we were all looking forward to Wibby having babies some day but she never did. Animal husbandry wasn't our long suit.

Normally, praying mantises only live for a year but (no doubt from being a spoiled, indoor bug and all) by a year and a half Wibby was big and fat and as healthy as any bug you'd ever want to meet. The last time we checked she was between nine and ten inches long. It was hard to measure her more exactly than that because she'd always hop on the ruler. I guess to Wibby a stick was a stick.

She was friendly and loved to crawl all over kids. If you held something out to her, she'd snatch it from your hand, check it out, then throw it down — so that was cool. She did bite Charles a couple times but what else is new? If we were smart, we'd have followed her lead and gotten rid of that idiot in the beginning.

Then one day I got home from school and, just like every afternoon, went into my room to say "Hi" to The Wib. There she was, curled up in the bottom of her house, dead. I was devastated. Picking her up and cradling her lifeless body in the palm of my hand, I took her into the kitchen to tell my mother. I'll never forget Mom turning from the kitchen sink, drying her hands with a dishtowel and looking down at poor Wibby. She was upset too.

"Aw, honey, I'm so sorry. She seemed fine just a few minutes ago when I was in there spraying..."

Her voice trailed off as she thought about it. Then an "Oh my God" look came over her face as — bringing her hand up to cover her mouth in horror —

she thought about it some more. Girls never *think about it* until it's too late. I'm surprised they let them drive cars. Mom broke into tears.

It was in fact, common practice back in those days for Moms to, for no apparent reason, grab a can of toxic aerosol and wander through the house indiscriminately killing anything smaller than a kid. Of course it's still common practice for girls to *not think*. I felt bad for her. It wasn't really Mom's fault she'd been plagued with latent Nazi tendencies — no doubt inherited from my great grandmother.

Truth be told, Wibby was *so* cool that she'd simply *ceased being a bug*. She had become just another member of the family — a non-bug — and it cost her dearly. I think she understood the risks of being *just another kid* but tended to keep stuff like that to herself — just one more trait she and Dave's Aunt Connie had in common. That's how cool she was.

I felt bad for Mom. I felt bad for Wibby, nestled in my hand — still praying — and I felt bad for me. After all, *Mom* was *my Mom. My* responsibility. On top of everything else, *I* would have to break the news of what she'd done to the rest of the guys.

The Eggless Club took it pretty hard — especially Dave's Aunt Connie. Unlike the rest of us, Wibby was the only bug Dave's Aunt Connie had ever truly cared for. A dark cloud hung over our clubhouse.

Initially we planned to bury Wibby beside the clubhouse in the field of great weeds she loved so much but that just didn't seem good enough. Not for The Wib. Instead Wibby would *Lie In State* overnight while we put the word out.

The next morning, kids came from two and three neighborhoods away. There must have been more than thirty in all (I couldn't tell, I was having a hard time seeing) all coming to pay their last respects. Everybody knew The Wib. She was much loved.

Eddie had donated his model Viking ship and Dave's Aunt Connie had spent half the night crying and outfitting the vessel with a tiny new sail embroidered with simply "Wibby". I placed Wibby in the boat and we all trudged off to Alum Creek.

Moving slowly, silently, the procession followed the drainage ditch to a small clearing along the riverbank where we gathered for the ceremony. In turn we passed by for one last look at Wibby — each contributing small tokens of ballast to the Viking ship's bilge. A buffalo-head nickel. A cat's eye marble. A really cool hand from an antique clock...and so on. I added my favorite arrowhead. Dave's Aunt Connie took off her genuine gold ring and placed it right on top of Wibby. Then, setting the boat at the water's edge, we all said a few words.

Bill talked about how much Wibby was loved and how much we would all miss her. Bobby said if she had a number, we'd retire it. I reminded the group that while most people think *if you've seen one praying mantis then you've seen them all*, we all knew there would never be another Wibby. Dave's Aunt Connie tried to say a little something but collapsed to the ground sobbing, inconsolable.

Don produced a small bottle labeled "lamp oil" from which I poured a generous amount into the boat before dousing the sail. Bill handed me a box of kitchen matches which, after placing a few matches at each end of the boat and arranging others along the gunwales, I passed to Eddie. He'd spent a lot of time building that model — he should have the honor of lighting it — but Eddie turned and graciously offered the matches to Dave's Aunt Connie instead. She needed to do something.

Pulling her long hair back behind her ears, Dave's Aunt Connie threw back her shoulders and accepted the matches. Knelt down behind the Viking ship, hands trembling, she lit a match and touched it to the boat containing Wibby and her treasures. The flame took, slowly at first, but within a few seconds it transformed the boat into a small inferno. Dave's Aunt Connie said, "Good-bye Wib," and with that, she gently shoved the tiny ship out to sea.

Not a dry eye could be found along that riverbank as an ethereal quiet settled over the gathering of mourners who had come to bid farewell to their good friend. We stood watching in silence as the boat drifted downstream with the current — flames leaping toward the heavens from within a cloud of billowing black smoke. I heard Dave's Aunt Connie say, almost to herself, "I love you Wibby."

As the tiny vessel neared the river bend the melted hull collapsed under its own weight and Wibby, her Viking ship and her treasure sank to the bottom of Alum Creek — the creek that flowed all the way to the rest of the world. The flames went out. The smoke drifted off in one final puff. Our Wibby was gone.

So it was that Bobby Stafford and I found ourselves standing on the southwest shore of Paradise Island looking at the brand new praying mantis egg. A symbol, not only of the fragility of our existence, but also of the eternal nature of life — the hope of babies yet unborn. We were both having a hard time seeing. We missed our Wibby.

"She would have liked it here."

"Yeah, she would have liked it here."

I snapped the weed off above and below the egg and tucked the brand new Wibby egg into my ammo pouch loaded with sweet smelling raspberries.

Only then did we notice the rest of the guys farther up the shore, standing on a sand bar jutting out from Paradise Island toward the opposite bank. We hadn't realized it but evidently they'd been calling to us for a while, wondering what we could possibly be doing. Why we'd been standing there in one spot for so long. We continued up the coast.

Nearing the others, it was obvious by their casual demeanor that Paradise Island was devoid of dinosaurs. Wino had indeed wiped them out. None of us had ever actually seen a real dinosaur up close and personal and we wouldn't that day either. If it's possible to be relieved and disappointed at the same time then that's what we were. Upon seeing us coming to join them, Don, Dave, Jack Cassidi and Dave's Aunt Connie resumed their task of collecting driftwood and stacking it near the water's edge at the end of the sandy point in preparation for a celebratory campfire.

Upon rejoining the others Bobby and I added our finds to the bounty already piled on a big flat rock that Don and Dave had dragged out to the point.

Having found a blackberry bush themselves, Dave and his Aunt Connie had collected even more berries than Bobby and I. Not only that but, with Don holding him up high enough, Jack Cassidi managed to pick three ripe papaws. Papaws aren't all that good just raw like that — not as good as when they're baked in a pie anyway. They kinda taste like smushy bananas mixed with papaya but they'll keep you alive.

Then I presented everyone with our brand new Wibby egg. It was a bittersweet moment.

Dave — by virtue of his old man knowing so much about such things — was delegated the task of starting the fire. Dave's Aunt Connie busied herself carving up the papaws (they're full of seeds you know) and berries, preparing a feast — stopping from time to time to pull out the urethane-looking orb she'd stashed in her top pocket, near her heart for safe keeping.

Dissatisfied with his spear point, Bobby sat sharpening it to later re-harden (Indian style) over the campfire. Don had seen a buckeye tree back in the woods and, grabbing his spear, went to gather some buckeyes. In the meantime I took Jack Cassidi with me to explore the beach in more detail.

What passed for a beach was littered with clams and clamshells. I told Jack you could eat them but after opening one he said they were way too gross. I suppose I should have prefaced that with a warning about never sticking your finger into a clam's mouth. They'll bite you, you know, and are reticent to let go.

Noticing that the other guys had collected in a circle back at the campfire, we rejoined the group. Once there, Don told Jack Cassidi to go and stand guard at the edge of the trees so the rest of us could talk about him in private and, though somewhat uneasy about the whole idea, Jack Cassidi picked up his spear and followed orders.

In the course of our discussion we determined that Jack Cassidi was indeed a Cassidi brother — that in itself didn't bode all that well. On the other hand, of all the Cassidi brothers, he was easily the most likeable. We all agreed he wasn't much of a ball player. On the other hand, he'd been an integral part of Bobby's and my foray into the pre-Civil War buried-treasure-salving business. That the operation had failed so miserably wasn't exactly all Jack Cassidi's fault. That, plus the fact that he was even here, demonstrated an adventurous aspect to his nature that we hadn't really appreciated or expected. That, in and of itself, was a highly regarded virtue considered crucial by the Eggless Club.

He had been quiet when he needed to be on the way here and hadn't fallen off the King Kong Bridge. We'd probably still be fishing Charles out of the drink. I wonder now what poor Jack Cassidi must have been thinking — knowing we were talking about him but not knowing we were laughing about Charles. Even now Jack Cassidi, without questioning orders, stood sentinel along the tree line. The honest truth was, we all kinda liked the little guy too. When all was said and done the motion to allow Jack Cassidi into the Eggless Club was agreed upon. The vote — unanimous.

We called Jack Cassidi back over to the campfire and told him our decision. His demeanor went from one of confusion and paranoia to that of elation. We then administered our modified Boy Scout Oath that Jack Cassidi repeated back with great pride,

On my Honor

I will do my Best

To do my Duty

And to obey the Eggless Club Law

With that, Jack (now he was simply "Jack") became an official member of the Eggless Club. Jack — the Jackie Robinson of Catholics. What we could not have known then was that our actions that day would pave the way for the eventual merging of our two neighborhoods — a union that would not only more than double the ranks of the Eggless Club but would also expand exponentially our overall circle of influence, both within our community and without.

The time for celebration was at hand.

16

Buckeyes and Bobo

To everyone's delight (but not surprise) Dave's Aunt Connie took from her bag of tricks six nearly Mom-made peanut butter and jelly sandwiches (lucky for Jack, Bill was dying at the dentist's office) and set them around the campfire. After opening each one, pressing the waxed paper flat and anchoring the corners with Tootsie Rolls, she portioned the wild berries and papaws. Let the celebration begin.

We all sat around the campfire feasting and telling stories — most of which Jack had never heard. Stories from and about Wino and Johnny Eyeball. The night at the Old Johnson farmhouse. Charles and his snakebite. Charles and his pocketful of matches. Charles and the nail in his head. Charles stuck on his own fishing pole. Charles this and Charles that. Any really bonehead move was known as a "Charles" in our circles — now Jack knew why. A Charles was a person, place and a thing. It was a verb, an adverb and probably a few other parts of speech I never really paid close enough attention to in school. Jack swore he'd never be a Charles.

We talked about the field where the Cassidis' house now stood but also how we no longer blamed Jack personally — just the other Catholics. All in all, I think it cleared up some internal questions for Jack and he promised to pass it along to his brothers when they got home from their religious sequestration.

After awhile Don said, "Come on Bobo, let's go get some more buckeyes — just in case — and bring your spyglass."

Naturally, Jack wanted to know how I got my nickname "Bobo"...so I told him.

It started a couple years earlier. Times were tough. Good drumming gigs were always sort of "feast or famine" and this was a period of famine. My old man picked up a part-time job driving a delivery truck for Westinghouse. Half the families we knew managed to stay out of the poorhouse by going to work for Westinghouse when times were hard. Think about that the next time you buy a refrigerator or a light bulb — I know I do.

One day — this being pre-Beatles and all — my older brother, Ronald (yeah, stupid name, I know) and I both needed haircuts. Nothing new about that. What was new was — my old man had borrowed a set of electric hair clippers from one of his buddies down on the loading docks.

Now, you might say that's no big deal but of course you'd be wrong. It was a big deal. Back in those days nobody had electric hair clippers — no regular people anyway. Until you reached a certain age it was your mother who cut your hair — maybe an aunt or the lady down the street. Even then, it was done with just a pair of scissors. What you got was what you got. For the most part it didn't matter how poor a job they did because, for one thing, you were just a kid — "you'll live" — plus, worst case, they could always comb enough goop through your hair to make it look good enough to get by until it grew back.

Electric hair clippers, on the other hand, belonged solely within the exclusive domain of professional barbers. Those trained in the black art of making your hair look even, even if your ears aren't.

Old guys used to hang out at the barbershop — whether they were getting a haircut or not. They'd sit around and talk about politics and how the Colts weren't the same since Johnny Unitas got hurt and ask, "How'd you like to cut his hair?" Important stuff like that seldom warranted input from little kids.

Where I grew up, going to the barbershop for your first *real* haircut was considered tantamount to a rite of passage beyond which there's really no turning back. A kinda scary deal, really.

But my old man was a drummer. A musician. An independent thinker. He wasn't about to be dictated to when it came to saving a couple bucks, especially when times were tough. So, determined to confront the formidable professional barber juggernaut, he borrowed the electric hair clippers from his buddy Eugene down on the docks.

Exactly how Eugene came to possess such a novelty is anyone's guess but he was known for having just about everything. No matter what it was, if Eugene didn't have it or know where to get it then you could probably get along without it.

So, how big a deal was it? I'll tell you. It was a big enough deal that when the time came for my old man to cut our hair — people came from all over the neighborhood just to watch. Aunt Frieda was there. Old Lady Stafford came over. She even brought a dear friend of hers who nobody else even knew but that was

OK. That too was indicative of the universal significance of my old man's bold undertaking. The whole scene, in fact, was one of festivity — for everyone but my brother and me. We didn't feel the least bit festive.

To a chorus of "Ooo's" and "Ahh's" my old man rolled out a big piece of felt onto the dining room table. Lined with pockets, it looked like a medieval doctor's kit — the kind of thing Boris Karloff would be slinking around with on a dark foggy London night. The pockets, in fact, contained not just the clippers but a special comb, and special scissors, and special adapters, all designed for use by professionals. It even came with a booklet (which my old man promptly set aside) explaining how to use all the fancy stuff. I half expected to see a scalpel and maybe a bone saw or two but the kit contained nothing as sinister as all that, so that was a relief.

Still, Ronny and I instinctively assessed potential escape routes. Of course, I knew my brother's first move would be to trip me so I scooted more to one side of my chair, jockeying for a more advantageous angle should the need arise — I wasn't born yesterday. The shortest, most expeditious route was out the dining room doorway and through the living room to the front door. Not only was it *too* obvious but it would also require getting past my old man — a sucker's bet at best. If my old man took just one sidestep you'd be dead meat. One lightning-quick lobster claw and well, you know how that one turns out.

The only other viable alternative route would involve diving under the table, emerging on the other side of the room, then making a dash for the kitchen and the promise of the back door. That would mean getting past Old Lady Stafford and her dear friend. I was confident I could juke Old Lady Stafford but her dear friend was decidedly an unknown quantity. My older brother had the angle on that one but my plan was to trip him. He would never expect that — especially coming from me — I'd been saving that ace for a long time. Still, even that better option seemed rather desperate.

Dad plugged the clippers into the wall and clicked them on and off a couple times — not unlike the executioner giving the chair a couple practice jolts. My old man loved doing stuff like that. As you might well imagine, my brother and I were petrified. Even my mother was a little apprehensive but she disguised it with, "Honey, don't take too much off the top, it's supposed to be below zero tomorrow."

"Below zero" for crying out loud. Less than nothing! That's another thing about school — if zero doesn't mean anything, they should tell you that up front. Oh no, they'd rather teach you not to say *ain't*. That's why to this day, I take expressions like "zero" and "do not" merely as loose arbitrary suggestions.

Anyway, that's where my mind was when my old man said, "Let's go Ronny, you're up."

Wide-eyed, Ronny turned to see my jaw dropped in exaggerated amazement — yes, I had learned from the master. Old Lady Stafford reflexively scooted her chair a smidgen closer to the sanctuary that was the kitchen door — she had kids too — and along with that I noticed any remaining hope drain from my brother's body like pulling the valve core on an otherwise perfectly good tire. He really didn't have any other option but to drag himself over and slump into the tall chair Dad had positioned in the center of the room. So that's what my older brother Ronny did.

That's what he did because that's what spineless jellyfish do. It was great.

There are many many up-sides to being an elder sibling but getting to go first isn't always a perk. This was one occasion when I was more than happy to wait my turn. Now if the industrial-grade professional barber's hair clippers were to become unmanageable and blood were to begin spurting from Ronny's skull, I would be perfectly justified in employing any means necessary to affect my get-away.

Ronny wasn't so happy about it — his anxiety increasing by the second as my old man stood over the table pondering which adapter to affix to the industrial-grade professional-barbers-only hair clippers he'd borrowed from Eugene down on the Westinghouse loading docks — low, medium, or high. Finally deciding on the 'medium' attachment Dad snapped it into place on the lethal end of the non-Johnny-homeowner-style hair clippers and, after a couple more practice jolts, went to work on Ronny's hair.

Ronny winced with each pass of the clippers, even though it didn't hurt at all, until my old man reminded him what his head was going to look like if he didn't quit fidgeting. After that Ronny settled and things proceeded without incident. Gobs of hair rolled off the razor sharp teeth of the clippers and before long my old man was in his element. Sure. Confident. Independent. Cocky.

The ladies were all impressed with my old man's ability to master the professional barber skill-set in no time at all — he was a "natural" — and Mom was in her, "Yeah, that's *my husband*," mode. Twenty minutes later the job was complete. Dad stood back, studied Ronny's head from various angles then, satisfied with the result, pronounced, "That ought to do it. Go on outside and brush off."

Before Ronny could get away, Mom grabbed him by the shoulders and twisted him to the left, then to the right, then back to the middle. She presented him to the audience for approval and after receiving a "tea party" round of applause — he bolted for the back door. Ronny wasn't in a hurry to get out; he was in a hurry to get back. He was dying to see me get mine.

Dad humbly took a bow as the ladies sat in awe of his *there's nothing they can do that can't be done* approach to plain living. The girls loved my old man, always had. We'd all heard the stories of how Mom and Aunt Frieda had nearly come to blows several times back in high school over my old man and how Mom had ultimately "won". I'm sure that's what was behind the subtle girlie smirk Mom shot at Aunt Frieda. Naturally, Aunt Frieda counter-punched with her own version of subtle glare from behind her coffee cup. Ah, you could feel the love. Of course Dad wasn't above twisting the knife whenever he could either. I think that's where I get it from, my old man.

Ronny came dashing back into the room, winded from his quick trip to the back yard to brush off, and plopped into a chair — happy he hadn't missed my turn.

Dad looked at me and said, "OK, hop up here, you're next."

Of course, the real threat was long over and I knew it. Leaping to my feet, I practically ran over to the hair cutting chair, tossing in a, "How's come Ronny always gets to go first?" just for good measure. The ladies all agreed it was "so cute" and that I would be a lady-killer just like my old man. I thought Ronny was going to puke. He treated me to a not-so-subtle glare — I'm pretty sure he got that from Aunt Frieda. Stupid kid, he'll probably follow in her high heels.

Now an old hand at the hair cutting trade, Dad set about his task like a career barber. That's when the telephone rang.

Mom answered it. It was Uncle Pete. Mom obediently carried the handset over to my old man but it wouldn't reach. Back in those days, talking on the phone meant being tethered to a wall or other stationary point so Dad grabbed my chair (me still in it) with one lobster claw and lifted me a couple feet closer to the wall outlet.

Dad continued cutting away at my hair as he talked to Uncle Pete about yet another fishing trip — this one to Buckeye Lake.

Where I grew up, you worked hard, kept your nose clean and eventually you retired, bought a mobile home on Buckeye Lake and spent the rest of your days fishing and enjoying an occasional visit from your grandchildren. It was never too early to start determining where all the best fishing holes were to be found.

Off and on throughout their conversation, my old man would stop cutting altogether while he strove to convince Uncle Pete of this point or that. Dad was getting fairly frustrated and I remember him standing there, phone tucked between his shoulder and ear, snapping the attachment onto the clippers; popping it off; snapping it on; popping it off, as he argued his side of any particular point. Finally, after adequate debate, they agreed: the best approach to angling small-mouth bass is to use "soft crawls" and, handing the phone back to Mom, Dad returned to the task at hand. I guess he just didn't realize the last thing he'd done was — pop the attachment off.

Still immersed in the pros and cons of soft crawls at that time of year, my old man cut a swath of hair completely across my head — down to the scalp! To make matters worse, it wasn't from front to back or from side to side — it was both! Just like that! (I could hear Wino's fingers snap) I had a bald stripe from the back of my head on one side that ran diagonally over the top to the other side at the front. I could *feel* it. It felt, cold.

Clutching their hearts, the women all gasped in unison — unable to fathom what they'd just seen.

Ever the poker face, Old Lady Stafford screamed, "Oh my God! Bob, what did you do?!"

For an instant Aunt Frieda was glad she hadn't been saddled with that bum for the rest of her life. Old Lady Stafford's dear friend looked like she wasn't quite sure if this was supposed to be happening or not. I can't repeat here exactly what my old man said next but to say it was all his brother Pete's fault. Pete and his damned "night-crawlers are great for small-mouth bass" fixation. Of course Ronny was on the floor doubled over in laughter, at least until Mom smacked him upside his stupid ugly head.

I was the only one in the room who couldn't actually see the damage — no matter how I twisted — but I will never forget the feeling of reaching up and running my hand through my hair. "Oh my God!" was right. I had been butchered, just without all the blood. *Sans sangria.* Even lepers get time to adjust to their fate. They get to see it coming.

What I've found is: grownups readily adapt to unfortunate events — so long as they happen to other people. What began as a cluster of horrified onlookers was quickly replaced by a mob of Benedict Arnold lemmings, all trying to hide their hideous smiling faces long enough to vacate the dining room. Dammit, it wasn't funny. It wasn't funny at all. In fact, it was incredibly unfunny. On her way out, my mother at least had the decency to grab my brother by the scruff of his scrawny neck and drag him with her — the grotesque Debil beast still laughing uncontrollably.

Now it was just me and the old man and he wasn't laughing — but I could tell he wanted to. Bad.

Finally Dad said, "Don't worry, I'll trim it up and you'll never know the difference."

Parents always say, "you'll never know the difference," when they know you're totally screwed. This was bad. You couldn't even make it into a Mohawk and that was about as weird as haircuts got back in those days.

I have to give the old man credit — he worked on me for the better part of an hour but when all was said and done he ended up removing even the *low* attachment and just cut it all off. That was that.

Naturally, everyone said it looked great — "you know, not everybody can wear their hair that way but it looks good" and that it was *"me"*.

When Uncle Pete arrived, even he said, "That's how we always used to cut ours when football season started — otherwise you'd roast in those black helmets. Football practice always starts at the end of August, you know."

Yeah well, how's about this ain't the end of August Petey, old boy, and how's about it's a whole lot

167

different when *all* the guys do it at once? Grownups would rather you think they are incredibly stupid than think they're the outrageously callous, unfeeling bastards that they really are for thinking you look ridiculous with your head shaved in the middle of the winter.

As luck would have it, the latest monster/sci-fi/horror/voodoo movie had this old voodoo lady who ran the whole operation. Her featured sidekick was a huge zombie guy with big glassy white eyeballs and a shiny bald head. His name was Lobo. I guess I could have lived with that nickname (he was after all, pretty cool — for a zombie) but that isn't quite how it played out.

My little brother was just that, little. Little enough that he couldn't pronounce Lobo. When he walked into the room and saw me for the first time, sporting my new "doo", he freaked out and ran from the room screaming, "It's Bobo! It's Bobo!" and — with lots of encouragement from Ronny — Bobo's the nickname that stuck. Done deal.

Having spent a lot of time traveling the globe over the years, I've found that "bobo" means different things in different countries. Some good. Some bad. Mostly not good. Anyway...that's how I got the name Bobo.

"Well, you comin' or not?" Don had been waiting patiently.

He could have interrupted me — but he didn't. He could have gone ahead and gotten started collecting buckeyes without me — but he didn't.

I said, "Yeah, I'm coming," grabbed my spear and stood up. When I looked around, Don was grinning.

Dave was grinning. Everyone was grinning. Once again I had relived that horrible episode in my life. They all thought it was funny. I guess I did too.

Don and I went into the heart of Paradise Island to collect buckeyes — just in case. Buckeyes are good to have around. Not because they're good to eat — in fact they're poisonous — but because they make great weapons. If you know enough about buckeyes then you know what I'm talking about. The truth is, most people don't even know what buckeyes are. Even those who do know what buckeyes are think they are little brown bean-looking things with a light brown dot at one end (making them look like the eye of a buck). While that is true — there's a lot more to it than that. Folks born and raised in Ohio are also known as Buckeyes. There are, in fact, only two jokes ever told in Ohio. What is round on the ends and high in the middle? Ohio. And, what is a Buckeye? A worthless nut! Both are knee-slappers where I come from.

But the real story of buckeyes is where they come from. They grow on buckeye trees. When they are full-grown they look like walnuts. Not walnuts like you see in the store but walnuts when they're still in their thick green peeling. The only difference between walnuts and buckeyes — when they're still in their peelings — is, while walnuts are fairly smooth, the outsides of buckeyes are completely covered with little spikes. A buckeye looks a lot like the spiky ball used on the chain end of a medieval mace and getting hit with one hurts — bad. On top of that you end up with about a dozen little holes where they hit you. Then the wound usually gets infected. Like I said — they're poisonous. As much fun as they are, parents are united in their opposition to any activity that might result in some kid getting clobbered by a high-speed buckeye. Where I grew up buckeye fights were verboten.

On the other hand, when it comes to raw firepower, few beasts can withstand an all-out assault by a bunch of kids armed with buckeyes and with a buckeye tree at our disposal it only made good tactical sense to stockpile an arsenal. Don climbed to the top of the tree to pick buckeyes while I began collecting the loose ones from the ground around the base.

So, here's the deal with buckeyes; you want the big green ones, not the brown ones. Once they turn brown they get really hard and start to crack open in wedges — releasing the nuts to grow into new buckeye trees. Also, once they're hard you can't get a tight grip on them without getting poked yourself so you won't be able to throw them as hard. As ammo goes, that puts them on the downside of the bell curve because when you sacrifice velocity, you sacrifice accuracy — any kid knows that.

Don picked buckeyes from the upper branches and dropped them down to me on the ground. Obviously you don't want to try to catch them — that's a sucker's move, befitting of say, Charles. Then Don stopped what he was doing and took a long look across the river. He was visibly excited about something he saw on the other side.

"Hey, man, come up here and check this out! Bring your spyglass."

I tossed the buckeyes I'd collected into a pile at the base of the tree and — well aware of how more experienced climbers function — followed Don's same route up the tree. Clinging to the branch next to Don I handed over my spyglass. Taking turns looking across the river (then back at each other) we could, from our vantage point, get a fairly good look over the hill beyond. There was something over there. We couldn't tell what — but *something*. Shapes. You could just make out the tops of them over the hill and, whatever they were, they appeared to be overgrown with vines — probably the nauseating kind that bees like so much.

Although we could only speculate as to what they might be, they definitely appeared man-made — of that much we were certain. We also agreed that, if nothing else, they were now our destination. We had a known fixed point to shoot for now when we crossed the river, taking our expedition beyond Paradise Island. It had all crystallized to form the next leg of our journey into the unknown.

Then Don just happened to look downstream around the next river-bend. From the top of the buckeye tree we could see a bridge off in the distance. It must have been the Watkins Road Bridge. We had no idea we were that far downstream. We could just make out two people standing on the bridge. They appeared to be wearing sunglasses and either scarves or hoods, it was hard to tell which, but either way it looked very out of place for that time of year. They didn't look like they were fishing. To tell you the truth, they looked kinda creepy.

Clambering back down the buckeye tree, we collected up our stash of buckeyes and hurried back to camp — keeping in mind you don't want to run too fast with a shirt-full of buckeyes. That's worse than running with scissors, again, ask Charles.

Once back at camp, we gathered everyone round the campfire then Don and I explained as best we could what we had seen. In the backs of our minds we had all been wondering what's next. Sure, we were going to cross the river but then what? Now we knew. Now we had a destination — that's always reassuring.

It was already noon so we had to be somewhat conscious of the time. On the other hand we now knew exactly where we were and figured we'd be able to cut a lot of time off of our return trip by following the river upstream for a couple hundred yards. From there we would be able to pick up our regular trails and be home in no time. In fact, we were kicking ourselves for not having explored this far down river long before now.

We prepared to move out — a river to cross.

17

Beyond Paradise Island

The first thing we needed to do was find out how deep the water was between the far shore and us. This in mind, I found a fairly large rock, walked to the water's edge at the end of the point and heaved it a little more than half way across. It splashed with a low, resonating "plunk". Deep water, you could tell by the sound. Dave's Aunt Connie distributed the plastic dry-cleaner bags with the tops ironed shut. Then we all stripped down to our skivvies and, after rolling our buckeyes up in our clothes (buckeyes and plastic bags intended to keep stuff dry don't get along very well), stuffed everything into the bags and tied them shut.

Looking up, Dave's Aunt Connie couldn't help but take notice of us boys taking notice of her standing there shirtless. I guess we were all (what can only be described as) gawking. She immediately spun to see what could possibly be sneaking up behind (preparing to pounce) but seeing no obvious threat, turned back to face us.

"What?" She was suddenly very self-conscious.

We knew "what" but we didn't say "what". The truth is we didn't quite know what to say. Since the last time we had all been swimming in Alum Creek she had changed...somehow. She was shaped different than before. Like Wibby, she seemed to have acquired...extra segments.

I suppose, on some level anyway, we all knew her hormonal abnormality would someday take command of her physiology. I'm not really sure what all we had expected but, no matter what it was, this seemed somehow premature. I guess a guy's never really totally prepared for a shock like that — like answering a knock at the door and it's the "real world". Poor Dave's Aunt Connie. Over the next few years her condition would get much, much worse. All in all, I think we adjusted to her affliction fairly well. We looked up and said,

"What what?"

"What are you looking at?"

"Nothing. What? We're not looking at anything. Bobby, you looking at anything?"

"I'm not looking at anything."

"We're not looking at anything."

We dove back into tying up our bags of clothes and not looking at anything. Those plastic dry-cleaner bags that were so hard to come by in those days and were intended to keep things dry and didn't involve looking at anything. Taking one last quick glance behind her, Dave's Aunt Connie shrugged her shoulders and finished tying up her stuff.

We then took any loose extraneous stuff, put it into Dave's Aunt Connie's big canvas bag and lashed it to a tree branch up high enough to discourage bears. Nobody had actually seen any bears in our neck of the woods in ages but then, nobody but Wino ever mentioned anything about seeing any dinosaurs either.

Parents would rather see kids get eaten for being where they weren't allowed to be than to have them walk around scared of stuff all the time. Plus, it's better to be safe than sorry.

We gathered at the end of the point. As with most things, Don and I would be the first to cross. We started by heaving our spears over to the far riverbank then waded into the creek. Once the water rose to chest level we swam to the opposite shore — pushing our waterproof bags ahead of us. Stopping just shy of the bank, Don allowed me to be the first to set foot on the land beyond Paradise Island. I've always thought that was really cool — pretty much what you'd expect from a future Medal of Honor recipient I suppose. Believe me, being the first one to stand on forbidden land is a rush. If you ever get the chance to do it — don't pass it up. We grabbed our spears and cased the immediate area.

"What do you think?"

"Looks good to me."

Waving the others over, we quickly moved out of spear range. They followed our lead and in time we were all dressed and assembled on the far side of Alum Creek. Although the hill obscured the view of our destination, we knew exactly where it was and moved out. One each. Quick.

Maintaining separation, we wove our way single file up the hill to the ridge where we stopped dead — looking down the slope. There we all stood, dumbfounded, gazing down upon something incredible.

Before us we beheld the ruins of an ancient temple. An archaeological discovery of tremendous import. Possibly the greatest discovery in the Western World.

The Mound Builder Indians had nothing on the culture that had constructed this site. That was the good news. The bad news was: the whole place was surrounded by tall sunflowers.

On the surface the ancient edifice seemed quiet. Serene. Unguarded. Perhaps deceptively so. Deceptive to the others maybe, but not to me. I knew only too well the possible hazard posed by the sunflowers. I'd seen it before, up close and personal. As we hunkered down along the ridge overlooking the remnants of a lost civilization — being careful not to silhouette — I was reminded of the possible trap.

A couple planting seasons earlier I'd wanted to grow something. I don't really know why I wanted to grow something but living out in the country, surrounded by acre after acre after acre of freshly plowed and planted farmland, it just seemed like the thing to do. The idea of working in dirt does have its appeal you know.

My mother had a small fenced-in flower garden tucked away in the corner of our back yard where every spring she would plant an array of different flowers — of which I could readily point out the marigolds. Yellow with maroon. Maroon with yellow. You couldn't fool me. To this day I can still identify marigolds even at a distance.

Mom used to have a hard time getting to the very far corner of her flower garden so she told me I could use about a two foot square patch of that. They call it square feet but it was really a triangle — yeah, surprise, surprise.

At first I wanted to grow a watermelon but Mom said, "No," explaining that it doesn't work like that. Apparently, watermelons grow on vines and not just one at a time either — I guess I had the wrong idea about watermelons. Plus, she said they would, "take over the whole garden." I have to admit, an incredibly slow battle of plants has a certain appeal, especially when *my* guy would be a vine. Unlike most other flowers, vines can be aimed you know — so I can only assume she was reticent to labor under such disadvantage. She knew me too well.

After tossing out a couple other edible choices, Mom insisted — whatever I picked had to be a flower. Even bound by such a sweeping, arbitrary limitation, it struck me. Actually it was a no-brainer — Venus FlyTraps! I can't believe I'd wanted watermelons. What must I have been thinking? It just goes to show you what can happen if you don't think stuff through. Of course — Venus FlyTraps. Say it. The name alone is enough to sell those babies. Now there's an interactive plant a kid can really relate to. A down-to-Earth flowering plant with honest to goodness extra-terrestrial implications. They were easy to get too. You could order them from the back of just about any comic book worth its salt — right there between the "Fantastic X-Ray Glasses" and the "Giant 10 Foot Weather Balloons".

But once again, the answer was a flat "No". Oh, she gave me some song and dance about how we lived in the wrong *zone* and it wasn't the right climate. The wrong kind of sunlight. In essence: a transparent, shabbily constructed string of lies — presented so *matter-of-factly* as to dissuade even herself. You and I both know, my mother only knows *one* thing about Venus FlyTraps. The truth is, my mother is a girl — the rest goes without saying.

Mom said, "Here..." walked over to the bookshelf in the living room, pulled out a big picture book called

"Flowering Plants of the Midwest" and handed it to me, "...look through this and pick something out." So I did.

Do you have any idea how many plants flower in the Midwest? Well, it's a bunch. Most of them are really stupid with names I couldn't even pronounce (and I was always pretty good at saying stuff). Yeah sure, hang on a second while I quick, run out and learn some Latin just so's I can read your stupid book.

Oddly enough, the Venus FlyTrap just happens to be a Midwest flowering plant! You'd think that would carry some weight with a woman who not only prided herself on being logical but was real good at Scrabble too.

All it did was change her answer to, "I said no! Now, ask me one more time and we'll just forget the whole thing."

They always want you to ask them "one more time". What's up with that? Hardly conducive to forgetting something, I'd say.

After thumbing through pages and pages of mind-numbing pictures — I hit upon it. Of course. It was right there in front of me the whole while; I just hadn't realized it. *Genus Helianthum Annuss* or, to you more common folk — the sunflower. Perfect. They were big. That meant a lot of bang for the square footage buck. Keep in mind, this was way before Hippies so (with the exception of an occasional parrot) nobody actually ate the seeds back then. When all was said and done though, you'd get more seeds than you started with, thus affording one a Hamurabi-esque jump on the next planting season. In addition to everything else, they were cool looking. All in all, you really can't ask for much more in a Midwest flowering plant. I could envision field after field of nothing but Genus Helianthum Annuus; big kids in fancy outfits would be pinning them to their dates on prom night — automatic second base. Soon it would be Rockefeller, Getty and of course, me.

It was a stroke of genius. Frankly, I couldn't believe I hadn't thought of it before — even Mom thought it was a marvelous choice. Hint: Before you ask your mother for anything, ask her for a Venus Fly Trap *first*. Life was good — in the beginning.

The following day, Mom (harboring a better understanding of kids than I had given her credit for) took me out to her flower garden and had me tie a string diagonally between the two fences that intersected to form the far corner — effectively cordoning off my tiny triangular plot of earth from the rest.

She explained, "This is my side, this is your side. Keep it that way." She was serious. Then, handing me a packet labeled *Sunflower (Genus Helianthum Annuus)* she added, "I wouldn't plant more than about five or six or they'll choke each other," and with that, she went back inside to enjoy her housecleaning hobby.

Wow, talk about cool! I couldn't wait to get started. Of course, you can't really wrap your mind around something until you actually go to do it. Don't get me wrong, I genuinely appreciated the seeds but then, after thinking about it for a minute, it occurred to me — I had no idea what she'd meant. Choke each other? Five *or* six? That implies some sort of conditional logic, doesn't it? So, what are the conditions? Five or six depending on what? Parents love to do that, you know; it's a setup. That's how they get you to ask a bunch of really dumb questions so they can tell you to "use your brain" or "try using your head for something other than a hat rack" — stuff like that. Well, I wasn't biting on that hook. Not no *way*. Not no *how*. I'd just figure it out myself — that'd teach them.

Even though to this day it still makes me queasy to think about it, I ended up reading the instructions on the back of the package. With a name like Burpee they gotta be cool, right? Wrong. Like all instructions, they were worthless. I mean how hard would it be to show you how long one inch is, right on the back of the package? The folks who do that stuff could PhotoShop that baby on there in their sleep, right? It did say to water the seeds after you plant them, and admittedly I hadn't thought of that, but I would have figured it out after a few days of nothing happening. Oh, and they do say to plant the seeds with the pointy ends facing down. Well, duh. I guess they figure nobody knows the first thing about dragon's teeth either.

I ended up just poking holes about yea deep with a stick and planted ten seeds — arranged like a backwards rack of bowling pins — if it worked for the Berwick Dragonettes, it ought to work for Genus Helianthum Annuus. Then I watered them, filled the holes with dirt and watered them again.

Guess what, it worked great. Within four days they were all sprouting up out of the ground. Burpee should have me writing the instructions for those things.

I've got to hand it to the folks at the Burpee factory though — they make great seeds. I guess those guys are just so happy working at a place called Burpee, it's just naturally reflected in their products. Not only did every one of the seeds sprout but then they all grew like Great Danes. My only real concern about growing anything in the first place was whether or not I would have the patience for such a slow moving endeavor.

Every morning before school I'd go out and talk to them and every morning they'd be that much bigger — they even grew at night! Their growth was even more noticeable by the time school let out in the afternoon. Soon I had a really *small* clump of really *big* sunflowers. They were cool. So cool, I named them all. Washington, Madison, Lincoln...you get the idea.

One day an errant foul ball bounced up into the backyard and killed Eisenhower (a.k.a. 7 Pin) but other than that they all grew to be taller than me, and even Don. Life was good. Then they started to get...creepy.

Their heads got big and round with long skinny leafy looking things that came together in the front, hiding their teeth. They looked like those plants in the forbidden jungle movies that would spit poison darts or lean way over and snatch passing bwanas off the trail. They never tried any of that crap on me — because I was their master — but I could tell they were thinking it. Sometimes when my back was turned I could feel them staring at me. The taller they grew, the bigger and more menacing their heads became. In fact, their heads were bigger than mine — so heavy they'd hang whenever the sun wasn't shining. Creepy.

Then one afternoon I came home from school and they had all bloomed. I've never been real big on flowers of any sort but these guys were stunning. Big happy faces fringed with bright yellow petals. Smiling and happy. They looked like, well, suns. I guess that's how they earned the name sunflowers. I think Helianthum is Latin for "really happy stuff".

Every night they'd hang their heads and go to sleep but they'd be up again with the morning sun, rested and chipper, ready for a whole day of smiling. I was happy with my patch of huge beaming sunflowers. Mom kept saying how beautiful they were and how proud she was that I'd had the patience to "stick with it" — telling all her friends I had a "green thumb". Even my older brother was impressed.

One day near the end of summer I was out in the garden talking things over with my Executive Branch when Ronny came out. He just couldn't get over how cool my sunflowers were and how big they'd gotten. I guess I should have known right then and there he was up to something but I didn't. Never listen to a Debil.

He (the Debil) was throwing out compliments right and left then he hunched down for a couple seconds — scanning the heavens. Satisfied that all was OK, he went back to taking an inordinate interest in my plants. A minute later he hunched down again. After a few iterations of this, I too started looking up to the sky, though not sure exactly what I was looking for. Finally I bit...

"What are you looking at?"

"What? I'm not looking at nothin'."

"Yeah you are."

"No I'm not, it's just, never mind."

"You're looking at something, man, what is it?"

"If Mom wanted you to know, she would have told you."

"What? Would have told me what?"

"Nothin'."

"It ain't nothin'! C'mon man, you gotta tell me."

"Just bees, that's all."

"What about bees?"

"Bees like flowers, that's all."

"Yeah, so what? Bees like flowers, so what?"

"Think about it, man. Little bees like little flowers, big bees like big flowers, and these are really giant flowers so...you're gonna get really giant bees."

He hunched down again, looking to the sky. I did too.

"Oh yeah, it happens all the time. They just don't put it on the news because they don't want kids walking around scared of stuff all the time."

I looked at my sunflowers. They were giants alright, the biggest flowers I had ever seen. Especially Garfield, he was huge. Ronny stooped down and picked up the seed packet I'd posted on a Popsicle stick and stuck in the ground next to Truman.

"Well, it says right here, man. Genus Helianthum Annuus. That means 'ingenious herders of giant attack bees' in Greek or something. Oh yeah, they've been playing you for a chump, man."

I couldn't believe those bastards down at the Burpee plant couldn't have at least put *that* part in English! I examined the sky once again to make sure I hadn't missed something.

"I haven't seen any bees, just a couple little ones."

"Oh man, you saw little ones already?"

"Yeah, but they were just little ones."

"Yep, those are the worst. They're the scouts."

"Waddaya mean?"

"Scouts, man. Those are the little ones who go out and find stuff. Then they go back to their house and tell the others. That's their job, you know."

"C'mon, bees can't talk, man."

"Not regular, like us. They dance around and buzz and stuff. That's how they tell everyone where stuff is. We studied it in school last year."

I knew that was true. I remembered seeing it on Mutual of Omaha's Wild Kingdom, with your host...Marlin Perkins.

"Then they all get together and pick one guy and he has to go wake up the big bees. They usually just eat him 'cause they wake up really mad — then they come looking. Ok man, I don't wanna hang around so close — if you know what I mean."

Ronny walked off toward the house, stopping to hunch down and scan the heavens once more.

I called after him, "How big?"

Turning and studying the small patch of giant flowers for a few seconds, he indicated an invisible creature about the size of a beach ball — wiggling his fingers for effect — and said, "About like this." Then, satisfied he'd done all he could to protect his little brother, he went into the house. As I stood watching after him, I saw the kitchen curtains draw back and Ronny scan the heavens one last time — obviously concerned for my well being. Once again he demonstrated a wiggly object about the size of a beach ball then the curtains closed. He was a good guy, my brother.

I turned back to look at my sunflowers. There they stood with their phony plastic smiles — all the while knowing they were just setting me up to take the fall. The Genus Helianthum Annuus bastards! No wonder some scientist added the Annuus part — no doubt it was tacked on post-mortem. Lessons taught by dead botanists, in Latin.

Not only had my Presidents betrayed me (a concept I would later learn to take in stride) but even my own mother had been in on it. It was the same old story. First disbelief. Then denial. When I got to the anger part, time and space seemed to blur. Like being in a fog. All I remember was a chorus of, "Hey man, what are you doing? Hey, what's he doing?! Hey. Hey! No! Stop, man, don't do that! Hey! NO!"

The next thing I remember, I was standing in the corner of my mother's flower garden staring over the fence at a pile of Genus Helianthum Annuus bodies in the field beyond my backyard. They weren't smiling anymore. I had nothing more to say to them. I kicked some freshly uprooted dirt in their direction and stomped away. I was in mourning now, tears streaming down my face. I was in mourning for me, not them. How could I have been so stupid?

I wasn't halfway to the house when, through bleary eyes, I saw my mother come running out the back door — holding her head with both hands and yelling, "Oh my God! Oh my God!"

She knelt down hugging me and asked what had happened. I must have been growing up because my nerves were shot to pieces but through tears and sniffles I managed to tell her enough for her to get mad. Real mad. Johnny Eyeball mad! By then I had melted to the ground sobbing and Mom was straightening my hair like she always did and telling me to "settle down, settle down, it's alright, it's alright."

Then, exhibiting a strength I didn't know she possessed, my mother leaped to her feet and gave out a banshee shriek,

"RONALD! RONALD, you GET your butt out here, NOW!"

My mother *never* used that kind of language — she was mad! Coming out the back door, Ronny timidly made his way in our direction, guilt written all over his face. I don't know why Mom had Ronny come all the way outside because all she did was march over to meet him (more than half way) and, grabbing him by his ear, his hair, his head — everything all at once — dragged him right back into the house.

Man, did he get beat. I think years of pent-up anger and frustration were unleashed upon my older brother — the Debil. At one point she was even yelling about Frank Arcati, some creep who had jilted her back in ninth grade. Some anger transference thing was being brought to bear here and it was great — I think she needed the release. They say laughter is the best medicine but (trust me) it doesn't even come close to lying in your backyard listening to your older brother get the snot beat out of him by someone with the authority to do it.

Getting beat by your Mom is a lot different than getting beat by your old man. At least when your old man beats you, you know at some point the specter of a long term prison sentence will rise up to make him stop. Moms on the other hand, tend to live in the moment. They're not shackled by ghosts of future consequence. They don't have to stop beating you until they are physically unable to continue. Even then, some have been known to pinch. Ronny should have known that.

His better course of action would have been to go, and stay gone, until the old man got home. In our household you either got beat by your old man or you got beat by your mother — never both. This time Ronny got both.

Later that evening as I lay in my bed feeling sorry for myself, Ronny came and stood in my doorway — my mother standing behind him. Prompted by a poke in the kidney, Ronny spoke,

"All that stuff I told you about the bees, I was just kidding you." Another poke and, "Yeah, and I'm really sorry." Mom looked over his shoulder at me — with a girlie smirk.

I said, "OK," and with that, Ronny yanked himself out of my doorway and shoved himself down the hallway to his room. I heard one more "Ow!" then heard his door close.

Mom came back to my room and asked me if I was OK. I told her "yeah" but I tried to sound worse. I think the beating helped. She told me to get some sleep — it was a school night — reminding me how I'd feel better in the morning. I lay there in bed just thinking for a long time. At one point I could hear Dad and Mom laughing about something but I couldn't tell what. Then I fell asleep.

Perched atop the ridge looking down at the ancient ruins, I was suddenly aware of the other guys trying to read me. I was, after all, the subject matter expert when it came to Genus Helianthum Annuus. They knew that in my younger days I had not only cultivated the beasts but had faced their threat and emerged victorious.

You know how in the monster movies where they always just *happened* to have one guy who just *happened* to have studied the species from which the monsters had been derived? Well, it's not as improbable as one might think. They were indeed fortunate to have me along. I knew just how to deal with that particular Genus of Annuus. Fortified by having just revisited that roller coaster episode of my youth, I looked around at everyone then back to Don. "Let's do it."

After passing around a silent "thumbs up" we moved out, one each, quick, in the direction of the ancient site — maintaining constant vigil against an aerial attack by enormous bees.

At twenty yards out Bobby and I flanked left, Don and Jack held the middle and Dave's Aunt Connie and her nephew flanked right — in preparation for a classic "V" assault. Don held up one hand and on a silent count of three we all stood and bombarded for effect. We reloaded for another burst. This time I noticed the rock I had picked up wasn't just any rock — it was an emerald! It's really bad juju to change rocks just before throwing so, on Don's audible count of three, that was my contribution. Yelling, hollering, and brandishing spears, with campfire-hardened (Indian-style) points, we moved on the objective. The sweep went smoothly and, after encountering no opposition, we met up in the middle of what could only have been The Great Room of the vine-entombed ruins. The A.O. was cleared and secured.

"Hey guys! I think that last rock I threw was an emerald!"

They all looked at me, wondering what was the joke. It was no joke. Rummaging through the vines about where it had landed, I found it. When I held it up for the others to see I realized it wasn't even the same one. This one was even bigger!

"This isn't even the same one!"

With that, everyone began poking through the vines and pushing aside bundles of foliage, exposing even more precious stones. You'd hear, "Wow!" and, "Oh, man, check this out you guys!" coming from every corner of the long-abandoned site. Once our eyes adjusted to what it was we were actually looking for, we realized the stones were literally everywhere. Not just scattered all over the ancient floor but also in huge deposits piled along the ruined walls. We had hit the mother lode. We were rich! Not just the richest kids on the planet but probably the richest kids in all of written history! What a feeling. It was indescribable. It still is. We couldn't even speak, all we could do was grin at each other and shake our heads. Rubies, emeralds, white diamonds, pink diamonds, every kind of diamonds. Jack said the real dark blue ones were sapphires — his uncle was a jeweler so he'd seen them before.

We began dancing around collecting the jewels and tossing them into a pile at the center of the Great Room. Then we all sat in a circle around the growing mound of treasure. We still couldn't believe it because it was truly unbelievable.

Bobby said he was going to get a brand new bicycle. Dave's Aunt Connie held a huge ruby on the back of her hand — like a giant ruby wedding ring — and asked, "What do you think, a little too much?" We all cracked up. I decided right then and there to buy a big sailboat, maybe even build it myself, and sail the world in search of adventure. My old man wouldn't have to work anymore so he could go too. He'd be a good man to have aboard. None of our folks would have to work again, ever. Bill's old man could quit filling plastic bags with small parts of specific types and quantities — he never liked that job very much anyway. Life was good.

It's a strange thing about untold riches. Once you have something...you have something to lose. That thought had occurred to Dave.

"You guys remember, in Sinbad, when they were goofing around in all that treasure and the Cyclops came back?"

It was a valid point. A sobering thought. All of this stuff might belong to a Cyclops or who knows what. Whoever or whatever owned this treasure must be big — and bad. A lame-o beast could never have compiled such bounty and hung on to it. We decided to gather what treasure we could carry and get it back to Paradise Island. Now that we knew where it was, we could always come back for more — at will. The next time we would have Eddie and Bill (assuming he survived his dentist appointment). It was a shame they had missed it — but they would still receive equal shares of the loot. That's just how we rolled in the Eggless Club.

After stuffing our pockets full with the precious jewels, we took off our shirts and tied even more into bundles we could carry. Don carved the word Eggless into the soft crumbling surface near the top of the longest ruined wall then, grabbing our spears and bundles of loot, we headed back toward the river. Barring one tense moment — it's uncanny how similar are the sounds of a twin-engine Cessna following the river and the drone of enormous bees — the hike back to Alum Creek was uneventful. Lost in our thoughts, we made it back in no time.

The operative word in "precious stones" is "stones" — at least insofar as crossing deep water is concerned. Stones are heavy. It wasn't much of a stretch to envision oneself weighted down with treasure, snagged on a Studebaker at the bottom of Alum Creek. Wouldn't the Crypt Keeper have a field day with that one? We considered building a raft to float them across but, without some rope or at least some decent twine, that seemed more of a long-term solution better suited for next time.

So, plan "B" called for Don and me to swim across first to retrieve Dave's Aunt Connie's canvas bag and empty it. Then one of us would swim back with it. After filling it with jewels we would lash it to the big chunk of log that lay awash along the riverbank — figuring with everyone kicking we should be able to float the whole works across.

Once again we all stripped down to our skivvies and put our stuff back into the plastic bags. Don and I threw our spears over and swam across. It's funny, but as we dragged ourselves up onto Paradise Island it had occurred to both of us — why not just toss the stones over, the same way we had done our spears? Duh. It was such a simple solution, how could we not have thought of it before?

I yelled the idea back to the others and they all laughed, smacking themselves in the heads, duh. Of course. We must really be slipping. Super duh. So, that's exactly what we did.

One by one they heaved the precious stones over to Don and me. During this, we couldn't help but notice that Dave's Aunt Connie's segment affliction had become much more pronounced just in the short time since we had crossed the river earlier. I surmised it probably had something to do with her lugging a bundle of precious jewels all the way there.

At the time, I had no idea how astute my observation had been — a misstep that could someday factor into not only the rise but so too the demise and eventual total collapse of a financial estate. Leaving in its wake the mere husk of the soul who would be its primary benefactor — knowing naught the source but solely the stench of dead albatross long slung round his neck. Left to ponder an improvident fate whilst scribing writs of islands and winos and other such truck — thereafter peddling them to unsuspecting consumers. Don't laugh, it can happen.

Soon the balance of the Eggless Club had crossed the river, dressed, and were sitting around a newly rekindled campfire alongside a pile of dreams. All that remained was to get home with the goods.

18

Going Home and Earthmover Tires

For quite a while we hung out at the campfire contemplating our futures. Vowing to — no matter what — stay together for the rest of our lives, our find guaranteed the perpetuation of the Eggless Club for all time. In many ways that was the best part about the whole deal. All things seemed possible as we spent the remainder of the afternoon on our new island. Paradise Island.

We wanted to stay on the island and we wanted to get home at the same time. We talked for awhile then all fell silent. The air was still and the sun felt warm. Off in the distance you could just barely hear the drone of an airplane but except for that, and the occasional snap of the campfire, all was quiet. Peaceful.

It was getting near time to go. We should pile our buckeyes and cover them with driftwood. It's best to keep them dry, you know. On the other hand, what had seemed important a mere hour earlier no longer held the same high priority as it had. Did it really matter anymore whether or not our buckeyes got wet? The truth is, our perspectives had already begun to skew. We really didn't have anything left to worry about.

Things were different now. We hadn't figured on that. It seemed strange, foreign. No, we really hadn't figured on that at all. From now on life would always be viewed through the lens of *before* and *after* that day. The joy of finding a pop bottle was gone — a delight relegated to the "not so well off". Those folks who still are what we once were. Strangers would come to mow the lawn. Only crazy, eccentric millionaires get to mow their own lawns.

I guess even the best moments of one's life come grudgingly, with an element of sadness. You know how every black cloud has a silver lining? Well, so too does every silver lining come with its own black cloud. Actually, none of that silver lining stuff is true anyway (I've looked) but that's not the point. Sometimes wealth has nothing to do with anything.

Putting all the precious gemstones back into Dave's Aunt Connie's canvas bag and running three spears through the strap, we would carry the jewels slung under the bundle of spears the same way African natives carry a wildebeest in the Tarzan movies. That really does work great you know. Gathering our remaining belongings, we took one last look around then headed for home. We would be back...first chance.

Slow moving but steady, our safari followed the river upstream and before long we were back in the familiar territory of cornfield at the edge of the Bolls farm. From that point we would continue in a straight line directly toward the water tower in the distance. That was the best route because just beyond the cornfield, Old Man Bolls had that particular year planted sod.

Sod is a not-so-fancy way of saying grass. When it's all done, people buy it — if you can believe that. People actually buy it. Old Man Bolls didn't even harvest the stuff himself. Instead, when the time came, other people did. A couple crews would show up with a big machine. The machine would go along cutting a swath through the grass, automatically rolling it up (dirt and all) into rolls that looked like great big Ho-Ho's except they had green filling and you couldn't eat them. They were really heavy too. Then guys would come along and lift them up onto trucks where other guys would stack them in neat rows. I did that a couple summers when I was in junior high for some extra cash — if you call fifty cents an hour extra cash — and it was really hard. You had to work fast just to keep up. Everything else about grass is slow. As far as kids are concerned — except for the rolling-them-up Ho-Ho machine thing — everything about sod is boring.

Having lived through the Dust Bowl though, Old Man Bolls was a big believer in crop rotation. On one occasion he sat us kids down and told us about it — that and The Great Depression — trying to instill in us a sense of strong values after he'd caught us stealing apples from his prize blue-ribbon apple trees. He wasn't nearly the storyteller Wino was — all of his stories ended with "but we lived." When we got older, he swapped story telling for a 10-gauge shotgun loaded with rock salt. Of the two approaches to instilling strong values in kids, the latter was by far the more effective.

From a kid's point of view, the good thing about cultivating sod on this particular acreage was the contour of the land. From where we stood the terrain continued straight and flat all the way to the base of

Bolls Hill where it angled upward for about fifty yards before leveling off again. At the top of the hill stood the Bolls farmhouse along with a huge barn and assorted outbuildings. It was the perfect hill for sledding and tobogganing in the winter.

With a slight rise at the bottom of the hill, followed by an abrupt two-foot drop-off, the overall topology formed a natural ski jump. By the time a sled-full of kids hit what amounted to the "take-off ramp" we'd be traveling about a thousand miles per hour. The trick is to not allow the sled to yawl while airborne. Whenever that happened the sled would hit the ground at an angle, scattering kids like an upset can of marbles. It was still a lot of fun though barely worth the long trek back up the slippery hill. That was in the winter.

Summertime brought a completely different form of recreation and we were reminded of it as soon as we cleared the cornfield and entered Old Man Bolls' field of sod. There, at the boundary between the two fields, buried under a heap of brush, lay our giant earthmover tire.

Bobby said, "Oh yeah, that's what I want, an earthmover. I'm going to buy my own earthmover."

Don and I were taking our turn toting the jewels and bounced them up and down — making them rattle. "We've got your earthmover right here," Don said, and we all laughed. Stopping to sit and take a break, the six of us fit comfortably on the giant tire.

Technically, we had stolen the tire but we didn't know it. It was old and worn-out. All the knobby tread part was gone. We had no idea that even old worn-out earthmover tires without the knobby tread part were still worth a lot of money — to somebody anyway. To us it was just one of several old worn-out earthmover tires we used to play on until the workers told us to stop. We naturally assumed they just didn't want us getting hurt — you know how grownups are about playing on cool stuff. We honestly thought that's just where they put them until somebody got a chance to throw them out — just like the regular tires stuck in the mud up and down Alum Creek.

One Sunday morning when the workers were off work — we got a brilliant idea. We all got together (because it took all of us) and rolled one of the gigantic tires to the top of Bolls Hill. The original plan was to roll it down the hill just to see what it would look like but once we got all the way up there...things got a little more interesting.

Dave said, "I wonder what it'd be like to ride down inside this thing."

Don responded with, "Will you do it if I go first?"

"Yeah. If you live, I will. If you don't, I won't."

Don was usually the first one of the Eggless Club to try stuff out. The rest of us would wait to see what happened to him first before we'd try it. That didn't necessarily mean we'd actually do it — just that it was actually do-able.

With the rest of us holding the giant tire upright and in-place, Don crawled inside. He fit easily with room to spare. Snuggled inside — encased within the thick rubber sidewalls — Don said, "OK. Ready," and with that, we started him rolling. That's all we had to do too — just get him started.

The first rotation or so you have to push really hard with your elbows against the inside walls or else you'll fall out when you're at the top of the rotation but after that, the physics take over. Once you get rolling, the centrifugal force pins you to the outside of the inside like a refrigerator magnet — you couldn't fall out if you wanted to.

Don literally barreled down the hill with the rest of us running after but we couldn't begin to keep up. It's like trying to catch a car — forget it. By the time Don reached the ski jump part at the bottom of Bolls Hill he had tremendous velocity — careening into the sky in a long graceful parabolic arc. After remaining airborne for what seemed like forever Don and his strange flying craft returned to Earth — skipping three times before finally settling down and rolling and rolling and rolling. Eventually he started rolling in increasingly smaller concentric circles then — like a saucer spinning on a hard surface — wooble, wooble, woobled to a halt at the far end of Old Man Bolls' field of sod.

We were running as fast as we could but it was still a long ways off and we couldn't see any signs of life; in fact we were all getting fairly concerned. Then we saw an arm stick out from inside the tire. Then another one. Slowly, the rest of Don began to emerge. Still running, we saw Don stand up and start walking toward his house. Then he started walking toward us. Then in another direction. Then another. Then he looked like he wanted to go in two directions at once before just falling down. When we finally got to him he was laying on his back grinning from ear to ear, eyeballs still rolling around in his head. He tried to sit up but gave up the notion and tumbled back over.

"You OK, man? You alright?"

Don gave us a thumbs up (but it looked more like he was hitch-hiking) and he tried to say, "Man, it was great!" but instead he said, "Gerfrzniblub vibsnebit," so we took that as an "OK." After a minute or so, Don managed to get his eyeballs to hold still long enough to speak.

"Man, that was great! You gotta try that, man! Wow!"

So that's what we did. All day. It was a lot of work rolling that giant tire back up the hill each time but it was well worth it. If you ever get the opportunity to roll down a hill inside an earthmover tire — don't pass it up. Even when it's someone else's turn it's still a lot of fun just to see them when it's over. It's the greatest ride never invented!

All week long we rode our tire. At one point, we noticed two guys sitting on a bulldozer over at the construction site talking and pointing at us kids. Even from that distance we could tell they were laughing. By the end of the day, whenever we got back to the top of the hill, they'd all stop what they were doing and watch us roll back down. They'd laugh and shake their heads then go back to work. I think they wanted to do it too but weren't allowed. They knew we had their tire but they never ratted us out. They were cool.

We were having a blast. I say "were" because on Friday, Charles found us. We didn't know where he had been all week — nor did we ask. The fact was — irrespective of where he had been — he was back. He'd waited his turn all morning and eventually it came.

We told him to hang on real tight until he got rolling but Charles said they used to do this all the time where he came from. Of course, on the first revolution he fell out. Normally the tire would have rolled down the hill unoccupied (and that would have been *it* for his turn) but we stopped the tire in time. We figured what *did* happen *would* happen and were ready for it. On the second attempt he didn't fall out. What he did was worse. Much worse.

Beyond holding on tight until you get started, there's not really a lot to know about operating an earthmover tire. It's not like you have to steer or anything. Once you get rolling — you're going where you're going and that's that. And there's no missing a big wide-open field of grass, right? Wrong. I suppose if I had to pick one thing *not* to do it would be: Don't go shifting your weight all to one side just as you're getting started. Well, guess what. Charles just plain got off on the wrong trajectory. One could say the whole run was doomed from the very git-go.

To make matters worse, after he catapulted off the jump at the bottom of Bolls Hill he touched down at a slight angle. Slight but significant. After bouncing a couple times Charles and his magnificent machine went into astable oscillation. If you've ever gotten a shopping cart with a "bad wheel" then you know what I'm talking about — at least if you can imagine being *inside* that wheel. That'll rattle your teeth alright.

To make matters worser, the tire finally stabilized by cocking up on the edge of one side-wall — like when a stunt driver flips his car up and drives on just two wheels, except it was only one wheel — the vector result sending Charles off in a long sweeping arc to the right. With respect to piloting earthmover tires: when all you can see is grass on one side and blue sky on the other — you're in trouble. I don't know if Charles knew he was in trouble but we did. He was heading straight for the drainage ditch.

The good news is: he stopped short of the drainage ditch. The bad news is: he stopped short of the drainage ditch because of a maple tree. I distinctly remember it being a maple because when Charles slammed into it, a cloud of whirlybirds came drifting down. It was impressive — I'd never seen that on a windless day.

So, what's after *worser*? As luck would have it (at least Charles' luck anyway) when he hit the tree he happened to be on the side of the tire opposite the impact and went flying across. Hitting the other side of the tire and ricocheting downward, Charles ended up in a tangled heap on the ground at which time the gigantic earthmover tire fell over and wooble, wooble, woobled to a halt — each wooble eliciting another "uunghh" from the Charles below.

When we first got to Charles and lifted the giant earthmover tire off of him we thought he was dead but he wasn't. He'd just been out of air for awhile. We helped him to his feet and, after we pointed him in the proper direction, Charles limped off toward his house, cradling his arm. The next time we saw Charles his arm was in a sling.

In the meantime, we ditched the giant earthmover tire and covered it with weeds and brush. We're still waiting for the heat to blow over from that one.

Sitting on the earthmover tire — joking and reminiscing about yet another Charles moment — we noticed Jack studying the huge tire with interest. He was dying to give it a whirl and we promised him he'd get to try it the first chance we got. It would go near the top of the list of stuff worth doing. We'd even hire a doctor to be there on-site — what parent could object to that?

After some discussion we agreed to go straight to our clubhouse to plan our next move and, grabbing our stuff, we headed out.

When we arrived at our neighborhood we cut through the field behind Dave and his Aunt Connie's house, as walking up the street armed with spears and toting a bag of precious stones (African wildebeest-style) would surely have attracted attention. Our worst case scenario involved stumbling across a bunch of big kids. No, the best bet was to get everything back to the clubhouse, get our bearings, catch our collective breath, and go from there. And so, unseen we followed our trails, continuing through the field behind my house to the Eggless clubhouse. Bill and Eddie were already there — waiting as patiently as could be expected.

Satisfied we hadn't been followed, we all went into the clubhouse, closing and locking the door behind us. What a relief it was to be home. Only then did it hit us just how paranoid we had become. Though Bill and Eddie were dying to hear what had happened, we couldn't even talk. Instead, we just started laughing. We had done it! We had done it and now we were back. We were back and we had done it and we had a bag of precious jewels to prove it.

Rather than trying to say anything, Don and I slid Dave's Aunt Connie's canvas bag off the wildebeest inspired rig and, each holding one side of the bag, poured them onto the table. They looked even better on a table than on the ground. Now they were real. Up until that very moment they were still liable to be the fish that got away. Not anymore. It's funny how paranoia works.

Bill and Eddie's faces lit up. So did the rest of ours. It was like finding the treasure all over again. The pile grew even bigger as we began pulling the jewels from our pockets and tossing them onto the heap with the others. Then we all sat on the floor with Eddie and Bill

Going Home and Earthmover Tires

and — all talking at once — recounted the soon to be legendary tale of our journey into the unknown. Last but not least...Dave's Aunt Connie reached into her top pocket and pulled out her brand new Wibby egg.

I wish everybody had this memory. The precious jewels piled on the table in the middle of the floor — all sparkling in a ray of sunshine — flooding the room with a spectrum of color. The Wibby egg was gold. Then it was red. Then blue...and gold again. It was special and we all agreed Wibby would have been proud of our achievement. She always was the adventurous type.

We explained to Bill and Eddie about Jack and how he'd earned the right to be our newest club member. They seemed genuinely happy about it in light of the circumstances and welcomed Jack with a handshake. Bill tried to say, "Welcome to the Eggless Club," (or something like that — it's hard to be sure because the novocaine still had control of his mouth). He tried to explain that too but that didn't work either. Jack hooked one finger and stretched his own mouth to one side so Bill could see he had recently been through the same ordeal. Jack was a kindred spirit. Enough said. We all thought it was pretty funny. Jack would be OK.

Our first plan was to say we'd found the jewels in the drainage ditch — freshly uncovered from the last rain. We were allowed to play in the drainage ditch as long as it was reasonably dry. It seemed like a good idea until Dave's Aunt Connie pointed out that once the word got out about our find, the press would be all over it. The next thing you know someone would be showing up with a piece of paper saying we had no right to be there in the first place. Who knows how that would turn out. Anybody could then just go out and discover the real site and claim it for themselves.

If on the other hand, the ruins were deemed to be of archeological significance — as we suspected — then she reckoned we'd have the judicial system in our corner. Basically "finders keepers — losers weepers". Dave's Aunt Connie was usually right when it came to legal stuff and knew words like "judicial" so we deferred to her wisdom on the matter.

When all was said and done, we agreed we would tell our folks exactly where we'd found the treasure, figuring you can't really justify beating a kid for coming home rich, right? We did decide to leave out the part about Stokes and Billy Marsh and Wino — that might be pushing our luck a little too far. Instead, we'd just say we had overheard it from some kids at school and by applying geometric logic were able to put two and two together and pinpoint the location. That's kinda what really happened anyway.

The real key here lies in understanding one's adversary. Most convicted criminals ended up convicted because they assumed, falsely, that other folks think like they do. In reality, that's seldom the case. The Eggless Club hadn't survived as long as it had without understanding that. We had Dave's Aunt Connie — the Clarence Darrow of our neighborhood — and punching holes in ill-conceived logic was her long suit. Even at the cost of an occasional girlie smirk she was well worth having onboard.

That settled, the next task was to divide the treasure equally amongst the Eggless Club members. After counting potatoes to determine the picking order we set about selecting our individual shares — taking turns picking, starting at the top of the order. Bobby was the last one to pick so he picked two, thus reversing the order, and so it went. Eight kids. Forty-three stones. We each came away with five — with three left over; they belonged to the Eggless Club general pool. It was a long drawn out process — believe me, it's not easy selecting from a pile of precious gemstones — but we did it and it was fair. Everybody was happy. The only thing left was to decide on the best approach to breaking the good news to our folks. Whatever we decided had to be unanimous.

While we discussed our options, Dave's Aunt Connie rummaged through our one cabinet and dug out the better half of an old bed sheet. Tearing it into squares, she handed one to each of us and we tied our goods into bundles — marking them as our own with a red crayon.

Ultimately agreeing that with numbers comes leverage, all eight of us would go *en masse* to each of our houses — starting with my house, it being the closest.

Dave's Aunt Connie rifled through her pockets and rationed out the last of the Tootsie-Rolls. We were all fairly anxious about this next phase — the final stage of our adventure. It was hard to visualize this last part. It's a lot easier to do stuff if you can picture it happening in your mind first but I don't think any of us had a clue what to expect. It's times like those when a Tootsie Roll really helps. And so we ate our Tootsie Rolls in silence — studying the anxiety blended with half-smiles on each other's faces. Thinking about what we might not have thought about. Any missing pieces to our story. Anything else.

Sticking out her hand to each of us in turn, Dave's Aunt Connie collected the spent Tootsie Roll wrappers

— she was a nut about keeping the tight quarters of the Eggless clubhouse clean.

Then with a sudden burst of resolve Don stood up, looked at all of us and said, "Let's do it."

Immediately, our confidence returned and — whether we could picture it or not — it was happening. Right now. Hopping up, we snatched our bundles of treasure and filed out to meet our destiny.

19

Sedgewick's

Weaving our way through our beloved matrix of trails, we emerged from the field of great weeds not far from my house. My mother and my old man were both on the back patio. It was Saturday so Mom was sitting at the picnic table embroidering something on one of those hoop things like Dave's Aunt Connie was always carrying around. Dad was drinking coffee and reading the newspaper. Everything was normal — good. Anything taking place would take place outside — even better. It's hard working *en masse* when everyone has to stop and wipe their feet at the back door.

At one point looking up and seeing us coming, Mom leaned over and said something to my old man and he answered her back. I have no idea what they said but it looked like this...

"Now what do you suppose *this* is all about, Bob?"

"I don't know, honey, why don't you ask them when they get here." Turn the page.

By the time we reached the back porch even my old man had taken notice. This was after all, the whole lot of us — plus Jack — and my old man knew better than to underestimate.

As we all crowded around the porch my mother greeted us with a smile and, "Hi kids. So, how was the campout?"

Just like that (I could hear Wino's fingers snap) — the first question out of the box and it floored us. Campout? What Campout? That seemed like a lifetime ago. It *was* a lifetime ago.

"Uh, yeah, oh, it was great."

"Yeah, it was, uh, fun, yeah, a lot of fun."

We looked at each other and all agreed it was a lot of fun. They *knew*, we could tell. Already they *knew*. Parents have a way of twisting information out of you like that. They don't miss a trick. The fact is they *did* know. They didn't know *what* they knew but they knew *something*.

OK, here goes. I plopped my bundle of loot up onto the picnic table, untied the knot and spread open the cloth to reveal the precious gemstones, exclaiming, "Look!" with a big smile. The whole Eggless Club was smiling.

After Dad studied the treasure for a moment he looked at me over his glasses. He was hard to read. He knew something. Sensing the pregnant pause, Bobby put his bundle up on the table next to mine and opened it saying, "Yeah, look! We've got diamonds and rubies and green ones...."

"Those are emeralds, and the blue ones, they're sapphires," Jack added — proud of the knowledge gleaned from his uncle the jeweler.

Then everyone started opening their bundles of precious stones and saying "diamond", "ruby", "emerald" and so forth — all talking at once.

My mother then said, "Oh my, those are lovely. Where on Earth did you get them?"

We all looked at each other — then all eyes focused on me.

"We discovered an ancient temple on...the other side of Alum Creek."

My mother's smile vanished. "You kids swam across that river?!"

Then a strange thing happened — my old man came to our defense.

"Oh honey, of course they wouldn't swim that river. They went down to the Watkins Road bridge, didn't you kids?"

"Yeah, we didn't swim the river."

"Yeah, no way, we went down to the bridge."

My old man knew something. Smiling again, my mother picked up one of the huge rubies and stood holding it up to the sun.

"Yes, they certainly are beautiful."

Putting her hand on my old man's shoulder, she smiled at him. A big warm Mom smile. I think I detected a hint of girlie smirk. Then without looking back (barely able to contain her joy) she went into the house — actually letting the screen door slam behind her! She was on cloud nine. All eyes returned to my old man as he sat studying one of the emeralds. He's a hard guy to read.

Finally I asked, "What do you think they're worth Dad?"

"Oh, hmmm, geez, it's kinda hard to say. I'll tell you what..." he set the huge emerald back atop the pile from which he had gotten it and stood up, "...why don't you boys go ahead and have a seat — you too Connie. I'll be right back." With that, he went into the house. He didn't let the door slam.

We all sat down at the picnic table on the back patio in the waning hours of that long Saturday afternoon.

Don said, "I'll bet your old man is getting a book on diamonds and stuff."

Jack chimed in, "Yeah, my uncle has one of those. It tells you how much stuff is."

After a few minutes Dave's Aunt Connie asked, "What do you suppose your father's doing in there?"

I just shrugged my shoulders.

Eddie commented, "I can always tell what my old man is thinking but your old man, I don't know. He's really hard to figure out."

"Yeah, I know. He's a drummer."

After what seemed forever, my old man came back out onto the patio, motioned for us to clear a spot, and set a big metal strong box on the picnic table in front of us. Picking through his keys, he found the one he wanted and unlocked the metal box. He opened the lid and after rummaging through the contents pulled out a huge diamond, looked at it for a second, then set it on the table. A little more digging yielded a ruby and an emerald. All three were about as big as your fist — maybe bigger. Then he closed the metal box and set it by the back door.

Ok, let's just say we were...dumbfounded. Looking at the new set of precious gems, then at *our* precious gems, then at each other, then at my old man then back to each other, around and around — we must have looked incredibly stupid. I noticed Mom standing in the window smiling...she knew something.

Finally Dad broke the silence. He looked at me but spoke to everyone, "You never knew my father — your Grandpa Jim — the one they called Pop. He died when you were just a little baby."

No kid likes to think he was once a little baby (especially around his friends) so I was hoping my old man wouldn't go too deep into it. He didn't.

"Well, back during the Depression — your Uncle Pete and I were just kids — times were tough. Things were bad all around. There was no work anywhere. My mother — your Grandma Pauline — was baking a cake but she didn't have any eggs. Rather than going all the way into town just for an egg, Mom sent me to borrow an egg from Jerry Bolls and his wife Sarah — they own that farm right over there," pointing with his thumb back over his shoulder toward the Bolls Farm.

"Mrs. Bolls was really, really nice. When I got there she said I was too skinny and made me sit down and eat a sandwich and drink a big glass of fresh milk — Jerry had cows back then, you know. Man, it was great — I was starving. She gave me an egg and I thanked her and told her that Mom said she'd send one back over as soon as she got to the store but Mrs. Bolls said, 'Now don't you go worrying about it, we've got chickens.' (Farms are great places if you like food) Just as I was leaving she said, 'Oh yeah, tell your father that Jerry heard they needed three men over at Sedgewick's and if he hurries maybe he and Jerry can go on down together to check on it.'

"When I got home, I told Pop what Mrs. Bolls had said — he flew out the door — then I handed Mom the egg. It turns out she wasn't baking a cake at all. You know, she fried that egg and split it between your Uncle Pete and me. I let Pete have my half but I didn't tell him I had just eaten a sandwich and had a big glass of milk."

Smiling as he thought about that sandwich, my old man walked over and tapped on the window. Once

Mom looked up from the table he acted like he was eating his finger and she whipped into action.

"Now, where was I?"

"You were splitting an egg."

"Oh, right. Well, Pop went over to Jerry's to see what's the deal. Now, Jerry had hired on a drifter who'd come through town looking for work. He used to do all kinds of odd jobs around the farm for room and board. His name was Emerson. Emerson Washington, but you kids all know him as Wino."

Admittedly, we'd all started to drift for a second but *just like that* (I could hear Wino's fingers snap) we were back. My old man continued...

"Well, the three of them went on down to Sedgewick's and ended up getting the jobs. They almost didn't though. Old Man Sedgewick was a mean, mean man." (It sounded strange hearing Dad talk about *old man* anyone) "Oh yeah, he used to work the men really hard — then he hated having to pay them at the end of the week. I guess he was a real son-of-a-bitch. Oh, sorry, Connie."

Dave's Aunt Connie waved it off. Her older brother (Dave's old man) had been a Merchant Marine so she had heard much, much worse.

"When it came down to it, Old Man Sedgewick said he'd hire Pop and Jerry but not Emerson. He said there were too many white guys who needed the work. I guess Pop and Jerry looked at each other then said, 'OK, never mind,' and went to leave but then Old Man Sedgewick said, 'OK, OK. I'll take all three of you, but this guy better pull his weight. The first time I catch him sleeping on the job, he's going into the next melt.' Yeah, Old Man Sedgewick was a real son-of-a-bitch. Sorry Connie.

"Well, Emerson never forgot that. He did more than just 'pull his weight'. He did a lot of jobs nobody else would do — either because they wouldn't or couldn't or because they were too scared. Emerson could fix darned near anything too. I know because I used to go down there all the time.

"Just about every day either Mrs. Bolls or my mother would pack a bag of sandwiches for me and the guys and I would run it down to them at the factory. It wasn't very far from our house. There's a spot where you could just wade across the creek unless it'd been raining — then you'd have to go all the way down to the Watkins Road bridge.

"But when it was dry out, you could just walk out to this little island, cross over it, and wade the rest of the way. Even the deepest spot was just barely up to your waist. That factory was so hot that a lot of times the men would just wade over to the island and we'd all eat our lunches under a big buckeye tree.

"I remember Emerson used to get really spooked by the salamanders that would come crawling by. I don't know why. They weren't very big. All black with yellow polka dots. I thought they were great. Other than that though, it was a really nice place to eat lunch. They used to call it 'a little touch of paradise'.

"After we ate lunch, they'd all go back to work and a lot of times I'd get to stand there just inside in the door and watch the factory in operation. It was a horrible place. Sweltering hot — even in the winter — and dangerous. They didn't make windows or glasses or light bulbs or anything like that — they made insulation. Sometimes they made rock wool and other times they'd change some stuff around and make glass wool. They're both used for insulation and they're made about the same way except the rock wool was a lot hotter. Mr. Murphy — he was the foreman who liked me and used to let me watch — would make me stand outside to watch whenever they were making rock wool.

"Rock wool was made from molten granite. That's like lava. You had to be careful and keep your eye on the ceiling for 'hot spots'. The ceiling was actually the floor of the second level and was made of real thick diamond-plate steel. Every once in a while the molten granite would leak out and you'd see a bright red spot start glowing on the ceiling. That meant you'd better run because it was just about to melt that steel and drip right through. That stuff would burn right through a steel-toed boot without even slowing down!"

My old man rolled up his sleeve, exposing a white spot about the size of a quarter.

"That's where I got splashed one time. Let me tell you, buddy, that hurt!" adding with a serious look, "That's what happens when you don't keep your mind on what you're doing."

Parents never pass up the chance to throw in a life lesson — a moral to the story.

"Oh, that's not all either. They used to have these steam valves. Everywhere you looked there was a steam valve. It seemed like every time you turned around, one of them steam valves would go shooting across the room. I remember the men were always complaining about how Old Man Sedgewick was too cheap to buy the good ones and how somebody was 'gonna get killed one of these days'. The ones he bought just weren't rated for the high pressure.

In fact, I remember one time, a steam valve blew up and hit this guy, Johnny, right in the face — darned near put his eye out. Whew! Man was he mad! Oh, he was hot and he headed up to Old Man Sedgewick's office. Everybody was yelling, 'Don't do it, man, don't do it!' but he just marched up to Old Man Sedgewick and 'Pow!' — right in the kisser! One punch — knocked him out cold. Oh yeah, Johnny was strong. Real strong. Used to play linebacker for Ohio State. Then he walked out and we never saw him again after that. Yeah, it was a dangerous place.

"And...not only was Sedgewick's hot and sweaty and dangerous — it was itchy. Real itchy. That's because of the stuff they call 'shot'. Shot is that stuff in fiberglass that makes you itch. All it is, is really fine, fine glass dust. I looked at some under a microscope at school one time and it's made of tiny little balls of glass — they look like tiny ball bearings. I used to get itchy just standing there watching. It was nasty.

"I remember one day we put some shot in Mr. Carter's coat at school. He was our math teacher. He was itching and got little red spots all over him. Then he went home for the rest of the day. We were lucky we didn't get caught — Pop would have knocked my block off...uh, I probably shouldn't be telling you boys this stuff. You too Connie."

While Dad was sitting there thinking about how he didn't get caught, I asked, "So what's all that got to do with these?" pointing to the picnic table covered with precious gemstones.

"Don't worry, I'm getting to that. Just hold your horses." My old man reached for a cigarette (Camel non-filter — Lucky if they didn't have 'em) and continued...

"So, here's the deal with making rock wool, glass wool, either one. It all starts with what they call the

215

cupola. A cupola is just a great big, thick steel bucket. The one at Sedgewick's looked like the big fat round part on the back of a cement truck." (We had seen those when they poured the concrete for Jack's house.) "First they fill the bottom of the cupola with coke — that's stuff that looks like coal but it burns hotter and doesn't smoke so much — then they put in a layer of broken glass (or granite — depending on what they're making) followed by another layer of coke, then glass, then coke, then glass, and so on, until it's full. Then they light the bottom layer of coke. That stuff burns really, really hot and it melts the glass on top.

"Once it's all melted, they pull out a plug at the bottom of the cupola and the molten glass runs like water down a trough. It spills off the end of the trough and pours down onto a great big metal wheel that's spinning really, really fast. It's the coolest thing you'd ever want to see. When the glass hits the wheel it looks like the world's biggest sparkler. I used to stand there and just watch it for hours. The sparks are actually really thin strands of glass fibers that harden right off the bat and float down to the ground. It looks just like cotton candy — except you can't eat it. I tried once. It tastes like crap and it's really crunchy so if you ever get the chance to taste it — don't.

"Just before it hits the ground, there's a huge fan that blows the fluffy stuff — that's the 'wool' part — onto a metal conveyer belt inside what they call the 'wind box'. The stuff that isn't fluffy — that's what they call 'slag' — is too heavy for the fan to blow and it just falls straight onto the ground.

"Now, the conveyer belt is made from what looks like a bunch of bicycle chains all side by side so it's full of holes. The shot that's left in the wool all bounces down through those holes so by the time the wool comes out at the far end of the wind box, it's nice and clean and fluffy. Nothing but cotton candy looking stuff.

"When the trough runs dry the next layer of coke catches on fire and the whole thing starts over again — that's the next batch or what they call the next 'melt'. As long as you keep adding layers of coke and glass to the cupola it keeps on cooking — all day and all night. Seven days a week.

"The problem is, after a couple weeks the wind box gets caked with shot. It gets so full in fact, the belt quits moving — just grinds to a halt. Plus, the cupola gets a thick layer of burnt glass all the way around the inside. It gets about four inches thick — even thicker on the bottom. So, they used to shut down the plant every other Sunday night and clean it all up. What they called the 'maintenance shift'. That's when everything was quiet. The maintenance shift paid time-and-a-half too.

"But still, no one wanted to work it. For one thing it was always on a Sunday night. But more than that, it wasn't considered overtime until you worked the next Friday and even then Old Man Sedgewick didn't like paying up when the time came. He'd say 'The finance department must not have figured it in so you'll get it on your next paycheck' and stuff like that. Old Man Sedgewick *was* the finance department. Somehow, getting paid a month later for overtime you worked today kinda takes the shine off of it.

"If you complained then Old Man Sedgewick would say things like, 'Hey, you're lucky to have a job,' and, 'If you don't like it, there are plenty of guys out there who'll gladly take your place.'

"Guys don't like hearing that — even if it is true. That's no way to treat hardworking men and nobody ever worked harder than Pop, Emerson, and Jerry Bolls. Nobody."

20

The Hardest Job

Appearing at the window again, Mom wore a big smile but I could tell she'd been crying tears of joy. She tapped on the glass and when my old man looked up, she pointed to the clock over the stove and held up five fingers. Dad didn't say anything — he just glanced at his wristwatch and went back to his story.

"Where was I?"

"You were talking about overtime."

"Oh, yeah. Of all the jobs in that sweatshop, the two hardest were on the maintenance shift. The second hardest job was cleaning out the wind box. Everyone hated that job. It was really hot and after two straight weeks online it would be absolutely jam-packed with shot — remember that's the real itchy stuff. Keep in mind, the wind box was about as long as this house. It was all empty on top of the belt but underneath was packed with that shot. Plus, the clearance beneath the belt was only about two feet. That's about as big as those drain pipes you kids used to crawl around in. A lot of guys couldn't fit up in there — even if they wanted to."

Eddie cringed at the thought. He remembered having to get out of those pipes — *now*.

"Well, they'd pop open the cover plate on the side of that wind box and it'd be just a solid wall of shot. You know, like on the beach when you fill a bucket with sand and flip it over. Then when you lift it up, you know how the sand just stays like that? Well, it was like that. You could write your name in it. In fact, Old Man Sedgewick used to always come walking by about that time and he'd take a stick — 'cause, you know he wouldn't want to get his precious finger dirty — and write a big 'E' in the shot. 'E' for Emerson. He loved doing that. Old Man Sedgewick was a real jerk.

"Ol' Emerson though, he never let it get to him. Nope, Emerson would hop right to it — happy and whistling — and that just gnawed at Old Man Sedgewick to no end. Once he got a big enough hole shoveled out, Emerson would jump up in there like a gopher and keep on going. It took two guys with wheelbarrows outside the hole to keep up with him. While one guy would be going to dump a wheelbarrow load, Emerson would be filling the next one. And, you'd hear singing echoing out of that hole for hours. 'Oh, the plant can't open till I gets done, the plant can't open till I gets done. Oh....' and Old Man Sedgewick would walk away rubbing his belly."

Dad kinda smiled and said, "You know, Old Man Sedgewick up and fell over dead one day. They said he died of a bleeding ulcer."

We had no idea what a bleeding ulcer was but it sure sounded apropos.

"But the hardest job? Well, the hardest job went to Pop — your Grandpa Jim."

My old man lit another cigarette and stood, thinking for a minute, before noticing we were on the edge of our seats. He looked like he was about to say, "never mind," — he'd do that sometimes, you know — but he didn't. After glancing at his watch for a moment he continued...

"Pop was a big man. Big and strong. Real strong. Pop never talked about it much but the other guys at the factory would tell me stories all the time about how strong he was.

"Like the day one of Jerry Bolls' cows got loose and they were looking all over for him. Pop saw him in the cornfield way down at the far end of the farm, standing there eating corn. Pop could see him clear as day from all the way up at the barn because he had an eagle eye. I swear he could see a country mile.

"Jerry and Emerson were working on the tractor so Pop told them to just keep on doing what they were doing — he'd go down and get that cow. Now, Pop didn't know much about cows but that never stopped him from doing anything before so he cut across the field, hopped the fence and went to bring that cow back up to the barn.

"Well, I guess that cow would rather stand there eating fresh corn than go back up to the barn. Pop tried pulling him. Then he tried pushing him but that cow was happy where he was and wouldn't budge. When Pop looked back up at the house, Jerry and Emerson were standing there just a laughin' — Emerson was getting set to head down with a rope. When Pop saw that, he just grabbed that cow, picked him up, and set him back over the fence. Then Pop stood there laughing when Emerson dropped the rope and him and Jerry just sat down on the ground. They couldn't believe what they'd just seen.

"Yep, after that everyone used to call Pop the 'Mule'. Mom said it was just because he was so stubborn. I asked him about it one day and all he said was, 'It's not like it was Jerry's biggest cow,' and that's about all I ever heard him say about it.

"The point is, Pop was big and really, really strong and everybody knew it. Don't get me wrong, he was about as 'easy going' as anyone you'd ever want to meet but boy let me tell you — you did not want to get on his bad side. He would knock you through a wall and make you fix it! He was real big and real strong. They told me *that's* why Old Man Sedgewick hired Pop and Jerry and Emerson in front of a bunch of other guys in the first place. There was one job that nobody else would do — even if they could.

"I told you how, after a couple weeks, the cupola would be lined with a layer of glass about four inches thick, right? And that was just the sides. The bottom was thicker than that. Now, I don't know how many of you kids ever ran a jackhammer — but you've got to be big and strong just to *look* at one of those things. Well, every other Sunday night, after the cupola had cooled down enough — don't get me wrong, it was still hotter than Hell (sorry, Connie) — Pop would hop up in there and jackhammer all that burnt glass out of there. Oh it took hours but when Pop was done you could practically eat out of that cupola."

My old man picked up one of the big rubies about the size of my fist — maybe bigger — and held it up in front of us kids.

"And *that*...is where these come from."

I guess it goes without saying we were speechless. Shocked. Amazed. Taken aback. You name it and that's what we were. We sat looking at each other. Then back at my old man. Then at Mom, standing at the window — tears of joy streaming down her face. That was just the beginning.

Don nudged Bill and said, "Look."

We all looked up and coming up through the backyard was Bill's old man. As he got closer we could see he was carrying an emerald as big as your fist, maybe bigger, and grinning like there was no tomorrow. Then from around the end of the house came Eddie's parents and Dave's old man (Dave's Aunt Connie's oldest brother). Bobby's old man came out the back door followed by Don's old man and even Jack's parents — all carrying huge precious stones. One by one they filed by the picnic table, nudging kids and mussing hair, each adding another gemstone or two to the growing pile of treasure. Oh, but it wasn't over yet...

My old man said, "You kids remember Fred Stokes' boy Danny, don't you?"

Stokes and his old man came around the corner and added more stones to the pile. That's the first time we'd ever seen Stokes smiling when he wasn't clobbering someone.

Stokes leaned over to Don and whispered, "I would have given you better directions but Old Lady Nettles grabbed you before I got the chance." Don just rubbed his ear. We later found out it was actually Stokes' old man who had signed the water tower.

So now we were, what? Stupefied? Flabbergasted? I'm out. You'll just have to come up with your own word here. But it's still not over...

We all looked up to see, rounding the end of the driveway onto the patio, my great grandmother and Old Man Bolls. Walking between them — that's right, I said walking, slowly and with a cane but walking nonetheless — was an old, old, old black man. There, bigger than Stuttgart (as Wino himself would say) stood

Wino himself. Now you can take whatever word you were thinking and double it! Not so easy is it?

My old man said, "We're really glad you could make it, Emerson."

"Oh no. Oh no. I wouldna' missed it for the world, Bobby." Wino calls my old man Bobby.

The gathering broke into a round of respectful applause, parting as Wino slowly made his way to the picnic table.

Reaching out an old, shaking, but still rivet-tossing-strong hand, Wino placed the biggest ruby of them all on top of the heap. Still holding on to it for support he looked at each of us kids in turn as the scene grew deathly quiet. He had that kinda mean face he used whenever he was real serious about something.

Satisfied he'd thoroughly scanned us all, Wino's face turned to a great big smile and he said, "Gotcha!"

And the crowd went wild!

Everyone was laughing. Not just "parent laughing", where they laugh so you'll think they think something is funny even though it isn't. Oh, no. This was the real thing.

We kids weren't laughing. We still had to go through the denial, anger, mourning, and final acceptance bit. That took about a minute.

Just the look on the other guy's faces — jaws dropped in genuine amazement — was the funniest part and I had no reason the think I looked any different. Oh, we'd been "got" alright, big time. You know, when everyone is laughing like crazed gibbering idiots, it's nearly impossible not to join in — even if you didn't hear the joke. Plus, if Wino was in on it, then you know it's OK. He had, after all, given us fair warning. Let's face it, it was a well thought out, perfectly executed plan.

The other guys had already started to crack. We'd done been got. Got good. Don was the first to go. The one guy you figured you could count on! We knew once Don folded, that would be it. Don folded. Then we all folded. It was funny.

We had totally and completely underestimated our folks' ability to engineer anything beyond a surprise birthday party, and even that was iffy. But this. This was perfect. No holes. No leaks. Not a hint. We'd been got good. Wino's story. Stokes and Billy Marsh just *happening* to be overheard saying exactly what we wanted to hear. And, "How was your campout?" Man, oh man.

Bill's dentist appointment was for real but his mother — to her credit — did everything she could to get it changed. Even when we were on the island, Mom and Aunt Frieda had been watching through the trees from the Watkins Road bridge with Uncle Pete's binoculars. Who would ever have suspected his mother could use binoculars? I later heard Mom lean over to Dave's Aunt Connie and whisper (Mom whispers like other people yell) something about getting to the age where "you need to start keeping your shirt on". Apparently her older brother hadn't covered quite everything in their little talks but her and Mom would "get together". I couldn't hear exactly what all Mom said but at first Dave's Aunt Connie looked surprised. Then shocked. Then really, really angry. When she looked over at us guys we all feigned stupidity — it wasn't much of a stretch. My mother's a rat.

In no time we were all laughing and joking and having a great time. Grandma and Aunt Frieda brought out trays of Kool-Aid, handed everyone a glass, and my old man rose to make a toast.

"First of all...I knew you guys could do it. You too Connie."

He stuck out his hand toward his brother and Uncle Pete passed my old man a five-dollar bill. After "popping" it a couple times (strictly for show) and validating its authenticity (strictly not for show) Dad stuffed it into his pocket. We kids didn't get the joke but everyone else did. Then my old man raised his glass of Kool-Aid and continued...

"Tonight we toast a great bunch of kids who set out to do something then went out and did it. Kids who exemplify the free spirit of kids all over the world — past, present, and future. I think I speak for everyone here when I say I'm proud of each and every one of them."

"Here, here!"

"You said it, Bob!"

"Yeah dass right. You know dass right!"

Tilting our glasses, we all drank to our trek into the unknown — our expedition to Paradise Island and beyond. Then, following a round of cheers and applause, the whole affair turned into a regular block party.

My old man, Wino and Old Man Bolls told stories about growing up around there. Dad said Grandpa Jim would bring him a couple chunks of what they called "burnt glass" every couple weeks. The kids in the neighborhood all used them for money. One would get you a baseball. Two were worth a bat or a football. Even a little one was worth a frog. Uncle Pete said he'd traded a little one once for a playing card with an almost naked lady on it (Oh, sorry Connie). Everyone laughed — they knew it was a steal. Uncle Pete was always getting cool stuff cheap.

They talked about the night they all climbed the water tower and scratched their names on it but when they got back down it was too small to see. So, Stokes' old man climbed back up and wrote his name real big with paint. He got beat for that.

Old Man Stokes said, "You know, every time my old man looked up and saw that, I'd get beat again!"

We all laughed at that. Anytime a Stokes got beat (for any reason) it was stand-up material.

The women all congregated at the kitchen table chatting about stupid stuff and laughing a lot. Mom and Old Lady Cassidi would establish a friendship that is even stronger today. Before leaving that night, Old Lady Cassidi stopped by our kids' table and said, "Thank you." She looked like she might cry. Moms are always doing weird stuff like that.

Later, as things were winding down, my old man picked up his diamond, ruby and emerald — returning them to his metal strong box for safekeeping. As he was taking the box back into the house I asked,

"Dad..." I picked up one of the pretty pieces of colored burnt glass, "...so these aren't worth anything?"

He stopped and thought about it for a long minute before walking back to the table.

"I guess, to most people they're not worth a dime. But me...I wouldn't trade them for anything."

My old man looked like he was going to say more — but he didn't. He used to do that, you know. He just turned and went back into the house, making sure the screen door didn't slam behind him.

21

Apology

I hate it when guys write stories then, when the story is over, they don't know when to quit. They go on to tell you how so-and-so ended up doing *this* and so-and-so went on to be a *that*. I won't do that.

I suppose I could tell you that Dave's Aunt Connie graduated Sum Cum Laude from Harvard Law School and went on to be one heck of an attorney — specializing in International Business Law — but you've probably already figured that out. I can tell you that Johnny Eyeball recently moved into an abandoned warehouse not far from my grandkids. I don't know what ever happened to Charles. My guess is, he eventually lost his ongoing battle with physics and he's dead now — probably took a bunch of innocent people with him.

I could say none of us ever *really* left the island — make it a ghost story. Oooo, scary. How's about Oooo, lame-o. So I won't do that either.

No, that's the story. It is what it is. Pretty much just one day on a spinning planet. A single drop within a drop of geological time — to most folks, "not worth a dime".

Sitting here at my desk, looking at my diamond and my ruby and my emerald — all about as big as your fist, maybe even bigger — I think about those days. Those big chunks of burnt glass are real good at keeping papers from blowing off onto the floor but mostly their job is to just sit there looking cool — a task at which they excel.

Oh, I've had plenty more. Lots of them. Over the years I've given them all away. Mostly to special people in my life. It was usually the same old deal, "Oh, nice piece of glass...uh...thanks," or something along those lines. Just what you'd expect from them what don't knows the whole story. After I'd tell them where they came from, the pretty chunks of burnt glass would usually be relegated to a sweet spot on a shelf somewhere. It's not the stones that changed. My oldest kid said it's kinda like the Rhyme of the Ancient Mariner except it doesn't rhyme, they're not ancient and there's not a lot of water to speak of. Other than that — it's spot-on.

Scientists say these precious stones will last millions upon millions of years and do you know what I think? Well, I'll tell you what I think. I think some time in the far distant future — a hundred thousand years from now, or two hundred thousand, or maybe a million years from now — they'll unearth these precious chunks of history. Oh, they might for a minute ponder the thin stratified layer of sediment that is me but their real attention will be drawn to the diamond, ruby and emerald — all as big as their fists, maybe even bigger.

By then they'll possess a technology that will allow them to read the stories contained within. Then they'll know about storm drains and Wibbies and long-extinct enormous bees. They'll know of hard-working men of all colors and jackhammers and TomBoys and Catholics. They'll know to avoid the planets and galaxies inhabited by the Johnny Eyeballs of the universe. All these things and more. Stuff that couldn't possibly fit in a book but can be readily stored in a beautiful piece of burnt glass as big as your fist — maybe even bigger — with room to spare. And if by then they don't possess that kind of advanced technology then give it another million years or so...they will.

In the meantime, I'll just hang on to my last three precious stones. Stones that, while they may not be worth a dime, are still no less valuable than the Hope diamond or the Mona Lisa or anything else you can't take with you when you go.

Whelp...I'd love to just keep on writing but all this time I've been neglecting the house and it's starting to fall down around me — not to mention all the other affairs of plain living. Besides, I have a heap of grandkids coming to visit this afternoon and hey...I've got a treasure map to finish.

Yeah, my old man's a funny guy...and now I've got it.

The End

230

Made in the USA
Monee, IL
14 February 2021